A Pelican Book
Cities: The

W. Harvey Cox was born in Northern Ireland and was
educated there and at the universities of Dublin and
London. He has been Lecturer in Politics at the
University of Liverpool since 1966. He has written on
urban politics, and is currently working in the field
of political history.

W. Harvey Cox

Cities: The Public Dimension

The city is citizens.
The city is the public character or
the public dimension of people.
– Theodore Lowi

Penguin Books

Penguin Books Ltd,
Harmondsworth, Middlesex, England
Penguin Books, 625 Madison Avenue,
New York, New York 10022, U.S.A.
Penguin Books Australia Ltd,
Ringwood, Victoria, Australia
Penguin Books Canada Ltd, 2801 John Street,
Markham, Ontario, Canada L3R 1B4
Penguin Books (N.Z.) Ltd,
182–190 Wairau Road, Auckland 10, New Zealand

First published 1976
Reprinted 1977

Made and printed in Great Britain by
Hazell Watson & Viney Ltd, Aylesbury, Bucks
Set in Monotype Times

And the streets of the city shall be full of boys and girls playing in the streets thereof

– Zechariah

Contents

Preface

At the outset I had thought of writing about the future prospects for Britain's cities. After some dutiful reading, however, it became clear that this would lead very rapidly into a quagmire of definitions and imponderables. I have therefore written about those aspects of our present urban situation which have seemed most interesting to me, in the hope that others may find in my interests and concerns some echo of their own.

The result should be regarded as a series of essays, some brief, some more extended, all around the theme of the city and the citizen in Britain. If there is one recurrent motif it is a concern that, given the scale of our urban agglomerations and the great problems to which their governments have to address themselves, we should give primacy to the fact that cities are comprised of citizens. In a democratic system, citizenship is 'the only thing people absolutely, involuntarily and perpetually have in common'.[1] As citizens, we require of urban government that it can plan, manage, promote justice and order, provide services to meet our needs; but also that it can give us reasons for what it does in our name. We require, as citizens, channels whereby the public character or public dimension of people can find expression; while retaining and enhancing the authority and effectiveness of government, without which our needs will not be met. Thus it is deliberate that I give voice to criticism *both* of insensitivity and self-righteousness on the part of those in power in urban government, *and* of the destructive militancy of the noisier of their fake-liberal critics. I am happy to be unpopular in both quarters.

As this is not a textbook or treatise I have seen no need to be over anxious about giving it a neat and tidy structure; or to apologize for the omission of topics others might have included. Furthermore, I am aware that I have committed one of the greatest of academic sins – to err and stray from the straight and narrow paths of specialism. Nevertheless I think it important to try to make connections, even if at the cost of being exposed to the criticism of those who have made their home in the specialisms invaded, and even if, as often as not, I could only claim to have hinted at a connection rather than proclaimed it. Lastly, I have shared the experience of many writers on contemporary subjects of finding oneself constantly outpaced by the appearance of new evidence and new studies. Valuable new perspectives on several of the areas on which I have touched have had to go unrecognized in the simple interest of somehow, some time, making an end.

I owe a debt of gratitude to numerous people. Chiefly to the authors whose works I have ransacked; the responsibility is mine and not theirs where I may have inadvertently misrepresented them. Many colleagues, students and friends have, for the most part unknowingly, fed me with suggestions. For too long, this book has been the most awkward member of our household; my wife has dealt with us all with patient care.

During much of the time this book was in preparation, the citizens of my native city have had to endure an upsurge of vicious and psychopathic brutality. A hope for them explains the dedication.

Part One   **Cities: Growths and Consequences**

Chapter 1 Retrospect, 1820–1970

BROADBENT: *Have you ever heard of Garden City?*
TIM: *(doubtfully): D'ye mane Heav'n?*
BROADBENT: *Heaven! No: it's near Hitchin.*
– G. B. Shaw, *John Bull's Other Island*[1]

H. G. Wells anticipated that the London citizen of
2000 A.D. would consider 'nearly all of England . . .
south of Nottingham and east of Exeter as his suburb'.
But what is more likely is that by the twenty-first
century, the whole of Britain will have become one great
metropolitan centre.
– Lloyd Rodwin[2]

In 1817 David Hume estimated that London had reached its maximum possible population of 700,000. 'There is a kind of impossibility', he considered, 'that any city can ever rise much beyond this proportion.'[3] The impossible, however, happened. Within a century, London, like several other of the world's great cities, had outstripped his optimum size by several times, and there were several other British cities with populations at or above his figure. Taking England and Wales alone, 20 million were added to the population between 1801 and 1891, most of them in the larger settlements. In 1801 there were no places, other than London, with a population in excess of 100,000; in 1891 there were 23, and these with London, accounted for 32 % of the total population. London exerted the greatest attraction of all; in 1801, 9·7 % of England and Wales's population lived there. In 1892, 14·5 % did. In Hume's own Scotland, in 1891, nearly 20 % of the population was gathered in one city.

As a judge of trends Hume may not have been very successful, but he may not have been so wrong in his reactions. An agglomeration of over three quarters of a million souls is, indeed, to be contemplated with respect. It is instructive to note how recent a phenomenon this is. The adaptation of our society

13

to a whole new way of organizing life has had to be rapid. Not surprisingly it has been an inchoate process, with many victims. And the changes go on, if not accelerate. A review in retrospect, of the process that has brought us to where we are now, may help in understanding our present urban situation.

By Hume's day, an 'urban revolution' was under way in Britain. This had two dimensions. One, the physical expansion of cities as their populations shot up and they colonized ever wider swathes of the surrounding country; and two, more importantly, the process by which the predominant way of life of the country, its culture, became an urbanized one. Urbanism, in Louis Wirth's phrase, was about to become 'a way of life', lived by most people. In this, as in so much else, London had long led the way.

'The unending story of London as a wen, growing blindly at the country's expense, begins under the Tudors and goes on in press, parliament and committee rooms throughout the nineteenth and twentieth centuries.'[4] If at present the conurbation houses some one sixth of the total population of England and Wales, one estimate has it that in the seventeenth century[5] one sixth or more of the adult population had at some stage in their lives experienced life in London. If, then, the dominance of Britain's largest city has grown greater over the last century, it was a dominance in the life of the nation which had gone on for centuries before. When Patrick Geddes called it a polypus, 'likest to the spreadings of a great coral reef',[6] he was only echoing William Cobbett a century earlier. Cobbett was acutely aware, in his peregrinations through southern England, that London was bigger than its mere physical presence. 'When you get to Beckenham, which is the last parish in Kent, the country begins to assume a cockney-like appearance; all is artificial and you no longer feel any interest in it.'[7] As for the city itself, it was the 'infernal wen' full of 'villainous corruptions'.

The cities of Cobbett's and Hume's day were, however, compact, if over-crowded. But this was changing, and it still is. In the nineteenth century, in physical terms the most visible sign of change was in the pattern of relationships between city centre and fringe. Great cities had always had suburbs, of course, but never quite like this. As Dyos[8] remarks, to study the suburb is to study one of the growing points of Victorian society. At the same time as the growth of the suburb, for both residential and industrial use, there was a change in the function of the city centre. It gradually shed its role as a general commercial, residential and industrial area, and came to acquire a highly specialist function, if not quite meriting Frank Lloyd Wright's accusation that it was merely a centre of 'sin and banking'.

From the middle of the nineteenth century, the city centre was already losing population. The population of the City of London, static at around 128,000 from 1801 to 1851, began a down-turn in the 1850s and lost 16,000 in that decade. By 1891 it had only a third of its 1861 population. Other cities experienced a similar trend. By 1871 every ward in central Liverpool was decreasing in population. The census of that year commented that 'the great decrease of population . . . is attributed to the demolition of old and over-crowded dwelling houses, for effecting sanitary improvements, for the erection of offices, shops, warehouses, for the construction of a central railway station and for the formation of docks'. The overflow and much of the general immigration to Merseyside went to the area of the West Derby Union. In 1851 this had 153,000 inhabitants, in 1901, 666,000.[9] In each of the intercensal periods 1861–91 the outer ring of London suburbs grew by 50 %, and in 1891–1901 by 45 %. In the latter decade the places with the greatest growth in the country were suburbs like Ilford, 277·6 % growth, East Ham 193·6 %, Willesden 87·4 %. In the same years the population of Birmingham rose by 9·2 % but that of King's Norton and Northfield rose by 102 % and Handsworth by 62 %. Liverpool grew by 8·8 %, Wallasey by 61 %. To commentators the advance of the suburb was one of the wonders of the age. The *Edinburgh Review* wrote in 1856 that 'Nunhead is fast becoming a brick and mortar wilderness. There is no prophet with vision clear enough to say to what limits the metropolis will extend

15

in 1881.'[10] The population of greater London in the late nineteenth century was growing at the rate of 100,000 per year.

To cater for the population and its needs was a host of small builders. At the peak of the Victorian building boom (1878–80) Camberwell contained 416 firms or individual builders building 5,670 houses, nearly all speculatively. They did not work in virgin territory, but in land already colonized. The form of suburbia in the first instance was created by the previous pattern of thin exurban development – the ribbons of Georgian villas and *cottages ornés*, strung out along the main roads. These with their gardens, and with the meadows and market-gardens between them, formed parcels of land sized suitably for the capacity of the small builder. Urban historians have demonstrated how 'our evolving cities are still governed by the ways in which earlier occupants of the ground divided their fields or settled their estates'.[11]

Economic advantage was for long the chief basis for changing the use of land in the cities. And with economic power went, to a considerable extent, political power. Hence the very physical shape and structure of our cities reflects to a degree the economic formations dominant at the time they were built.

Matthew Arnold's 'vast, miserable, unmanageable masses of sunken people', existed, most in housing that had begun cheap and nasty, some in housing which, as the cities grew, had nastiness thrust upon it. An example of the former type was the Brook Green area of Hammersmith, where builders ran up cheap and insanitary cottages on marshy land to house Irish labourers and their families. Examples of the latter were legion. Areas declined in favour due to the pressures of proximate industry or the rising aspirations of former inhabitants. One such area was that which lay in Paddington between the canal and the railway where, Charles Booth noted in 1897, the 'respectable' working class were already moving out.[12]

With the passage of time the great social divisions were becoming more marked in their geographical distribution. Northern Camberwell, in the late nineteenth century, had densities of 150 persons to the acre, and physical and social decay were already advanced. It had colonies noted for drunkenness and general excess; while in the south, in the vicinity of Crystal Palace, the villas began to climb the foothills of the downs, but at an easy 7 persons to the acre. In between was Mr Pooter; thousands of him.

It has long been fashionable to sneer at suburbia. But it was for many a necessity in terms of health: the air was purer and the water cleaner. 'The individual's retreat to the suburbs was often a personal response to a collective sanitary problem.'[13] For many too it provided an environment within which psychological satisfactions could be obtained. It conferred respectability, a chance to compensate for the frustrations of work, a nexus with the soil for city dwellers.

Transport, then as now, provided the essential link between areas of the city, expressed their inter-dependency and contributed substantially to the future shaping of the city. J. R. Kellett has shown how complex was the impact of the coming of the railways on the cities.[14] The building of great termini produced gradually a redistribution of land uses, attracting shopkeepers and warehouses, repelling residential and business users. Great brick or stone viaducts were built, usually to avoid the closure of streets. These served to segregate areas off, and encourage dereliction and marginal uses. The tactical manoeuvrings of the various companies led to the proliferation of mazes of crossovers and connecting lines in south London, east Birmingham and elsewhere, the purpose of each of which few, even at the time, fully understood. In 1900 railways owned 9 % of the land of the central zone of Liverpool, in Glasgow the equivalent of three quarters of the city's total size as of 1840.[15] The districts they divided off in the inner suburbs tended to become tracts of industrial wasteland populated by the most helpless poor whose labour the central districts needed. This was only one case of a recurrent pattern, whereby the costs of change fall most heavily on the already poor and weak.

Areas of bad housing close to the centre were thus largely a product of the rapid growth of urban population itself, but also partly due to the fact that the railways dispossessed people in central areas, and caused their crowding into zones cut off by the tracks from the rest of the city. In any case the lack of cheap travel meant that many of the labouring population were forced to live within walking distance of their work. The railway thus increased rather than decreased the compression of the inner city population, while providing a means whereby the middle classes could enjoy the benefits of space and light.

It was however only belatedly that the Victorian railways made any effort to woo the commuter. In 1890 only one in twelve in London's southern suburbs used *any* sort of public transport to get to work. Nevertheless, in time their presence helped to generate commuter housing beyond the inner ring – such as the north London suburbs with their large populations of city clerks. Only the Great Eastern actively prompted and sustained suburban growth, and its cheap return fares helped to make its sector of suburban London the fastest growing urban area in the country in the 1880s and 1890s.

The commercial and industrial activities carried on in the central areas needed to be serviced by a large, irregular and poorly paid workforce, while these very activities themselves tended to increase the trapping of the least fortunate of these in poor, overcrowded quarters. If this situation has echoes in the plight of the inner areas, especially of London, even today, so too do today's dilemmas of social reform reflect a seemingly perennial set of difficulties. S. D. Chapman *et al.*[16] show in their *History of Working-Class Housing*, how nineteenth-century reformers, local authority officials and philanthropists were constantly frustrated in their efforts by unemployment, casual employment, low earnings and general ignorance. More rooms, in the 1880s and 1890s, *were* provided, but only at the sacrifice of a larger slice of a man's wages. By then, there was already a division between those who wanted a policy of wholesale demolition and those, closer to the ground, who advocated a less insensitive approach.

Frequent, inexpensive trams and the growth of working-class suburbs provided some sort of answer, for the better-off worker, as they had done earlier for his 'superiors'. As Wohl[17] points out this was not a totally benign situation, since builders in the suburbs, free of official harassment, could use shoddier materials, and some of these suburbs themselves became crowded and in need of ameliorative action.

The failure of even philanthropic capitalism to provide adequate low cost housing brought the local authorities into the field as both builders and landlords. By 1914 their achievements, especially in London, were becoming impressive. But still, owing to the interlinkage of housing, employment, welfare and education, accommodation for the poorest groups remained an intractable problem.

The 6 census-recognized conurbations, that is Greater London, the greater Manchester area, the West Midlands, West Yorkshire, Merseyside and Tyneside, comprised by 1961 37 % of the population of England and Wales.[18] Compared with 1901, this was a reduction of 4 %, although the actual numbers of people resident in the 6 had risen. These conurbations were, however, very restrictively defined both in size and in number, omitting populous fringe areas and smaller conurbations such as Teesside. In twentieth-century urban growth the key category is the town of 50,000 to 200,000 people. In 1901 there were 61 of these and 21·6 % of England and Wales's urban population lived in them. By 1961 there were 162, housing 37·9 % of the urban population. The new towns programme alone promised the elevation into this range of no fewer than 15 or so formerly smaller settlements, as well as making lesser but still substantial additions to the urban scene (Hatfield) and promising the expanding of existing large towns into cities (Preston).

In the first 70 years of this century, a reasonable estimate would be that the urban area of England and Wales has increased by 40 % or so. It was between the wars that the greatest urban growth, in terms of land built upon, took place. In London, the continuously built-up area nearly doubled, although the area of the LCC had been losing population slowly since before 1901. There was little effective planning control.

The inter-war period saw slum clearance and new house building on a large scale by local authorities. Over a third of a million houses were demolished in the 1930s, while the LCC erected nearly 100,000 houses, half of them on land outside its own boundaries, which had been almost entirely filled up by 1914. They sought land, for example, for 25,000 dwellings at Becontree. These went to people earning under £4 a week – but not to the very poorest, for the lowest paid workers could neither have afforded the rents nor the travelling expenses involved in living there. This was part of a persistent and continuing pattern whereby public help has tended to miss out those in greatest need of it.

Despite this activity there was by 1945 a substantial deficiency of houses relative to the requirements caused by natural increase, bombing, immigration and clearance of decayed areas. In London County and Middlesex alone there was a 43 % deficiency of houses in relation to requirement. In 1945 in the Greater Manchester area an estimated 220,000 people lived in about 68,000 unfit houses, mainly over 70 years old. In 1951 in Belfast almost all the houses built since 1857 were still in use, plus 6,500 built before 1857. This city in 1951 had an average density of 28·9 persons to the acre as compared with 14·4 to the acre in Edinburgh and 16·8 in Bristol. Areas to the west of the city centre had densities of 95·5 to 280·5 persons to the acre.[19] The recent history of these areas is fairly well known. By the late 1940s, therefore, it was inevitable that much of the agenda for city governments would be concerned with housing, and, importantly, not just with building new houses on the city fringe but with demolition, redevelopment and rehousing of the inner, older areas where people were still living. The lesson, however, that mere energy was not enough when dealing not just with bricks and old mortar but with citizens and their homes, was to be long in the learning.

Meanwhile, the ties that had bound cities together were steadily loosening, with the weakening of the attraction of the city centre or central axis. Heavy industry, concentrated in large self-contained plants, located itself well away from the city centre. In the shape, for example, of car works at Dagenham, Longbridge, and, in the 1960s at Halewood, it in effect hopped over suburbia to start again on the edge of the country; and industrial estates, that invention of the Depression, were there too. Government and local authority inducements encouraged firms to see what many were disposed to see in any event, namely the advantages of what had previously been a rare luxury – plentiful space. New flexibility in transport had the same effect on industry as it was having on residential choices.

All benefited by the development, particularly in London, of improved suburban services. Before 1914 North Middlesex had been largely empty; but it was rapidly opened up by the extension of tube lines to Edgware in 1924, to Stanmore in 1932, to Cockfosters in 1933. This was based upon the shrewd commercial calculation that 15 million passengers a year could be attracted to use lines which, with short stops and travel at 25 m.p.h. between them, could reach the central area in three quarters of an hour. The advantages of life in 'Metroland' were held out, in perhaps the largest and best organized attempt to direct the course of city growth before the 1947 Act. Conversion to electricity of the railways south of London provided for that area a function similar to that which the tubes performed for north London. It was a development which, from the point of view of transport, was quickly to prove short-sighted. By 1939 the trains were so crowded that intense strains were building up on the inner approaches to London, while a growth of car-borne commuting from the inner suburbs was not entirely unrelated to the fact that trains reaching these areas were already full. Not for the first or last time in the history of urban transport, no sooner was an artery developed than it had begun to harden.[20]

The development of the petrol driven vehicle, and particularly the opportunities for personal mobility that it has given, as always in the first instance to the better off, has had a further impact on the loosening up of what had formerly been a tight urban nexus clearly demarcated from the countryside. In 1904 there were 5,300 petrol-driven public transport vehicles and

8,500 cars registered throughout the country. By 1926 however, while the former had grown to 100,000, itself a truly astonishing growth, the number of cars registered was 684,000. By 1945 this had grown to nearly 1½ million. By 1950 it stood at 2¼ million, by 1970 at around 12 million. In that year there was one car to every 5 people and the vehicle density per mile was among the world's highest.

The attempts in the 1920s and the 1930s to cope with increased road traffic had the effect of merely generating more. The arterial roads built between the wars were on the whole too narrow and, (until 1935) there were no powers to control ribbon development. Little attempt was made to segregate local from longer distance traffic; and in central areas, the cars poured into an already ossified system. London's Kingsway in the 1900s was virtually the last major effort to reshape a central city road system before the mid 1960s.

The car-owner exercises his privilege in terms of his greater mobility, as did the Victorian train-using bourgeoisie, only more so. In 1964, according to the National Traffic Survey, people in car owning households made 14·5 journeys per head per week and averaged 90 miles a week each, while those in non-car owning households made only 9·7 journeys averaging 45 miles. The miles travelled by cars (and taxis) rose in the decade 1956–66 by 153 % while those travelled by public service vehicles went down by 1 %.

The city centre's function has been changing in response to changes in the country's employment structure. The fastest growing sectors since 1920 have been in office based employment. One third of the total floor space in central London is taken up by office space. By 1939 there were 87 million square feet; this had risen by 1962 to 114·8 million square feet,[21] and the property boom was only getting into its stride. Oliver Marriott[22] lists 110 people each of whom must, he calculates, have made at least a million pounds during the golden (for them) years from 1945 to 1965. At the same time as this there has been similar growth in prestige hotel, entertainment and shopping provision. When taken with the colonization of former working-class areas by the affluent, this has intensified a long-standing tendency for the inner area of London to be the preserve of the rich and powerful and the poor and powerless.

The process whereby the city in Britain 'burst its banks' and ceased to be what Kingsley Davis has called 'truebounded', that is, where 'the political and demographic–ecological boundaries correspond'[23] has been going on for most of the time under review. As early as the 1880s the country towns of Harrow, Kingston and Croydon and even Brighton[24] were becoming attractive to the more affluent city workers as places of residence. There were northern equivalents like Alderley Edge and West Kirby. A railway tunnel under the Mersey opened in 1886 and paved the way for suburbanization of the Wirral. By 1911 an estimated 254,000 were resident in the Cheshire suburbs south of Manchester[25] while the populations of Manchester and Salford had stayed static. In 1933 with the electrification of the Brighton line, a belt of territory between London and the coast 50 miles away became 'commuter country'. The number of season tickets to Haywards Heath trebled from 1926 to 1936, while by 1936, 10,000 people a day were commuting from Brighton to London.[26] Since 1945 this colonization of the outer metropolitan area has proceeded apace, and between 1951 and 1971 its population rose from 3,500,000 to 5,290,000.

Thanks to post-war planning, the city in Britain probably now has more clearly defined edges, as a built-up area, than for a very long time, at a time when this definition has never had less significance in any other terms. The advocacy of retaining 'green belts' to control city growth and provide amenities had been going on periodically since Ebenezer Howard's day, and the idea was incorporated in the 1944 Abercromby plan for London. The official view, postwar, was that the green belts were to be checks on urban growth, to prevent the merging of towns and to preserve the special character of a town. In fact, the real object of the policy was to protect the interests of the surrounding countryside rather than of the cities. However, in 1963 the first official breach in the policy was intimated in a White

Paper which pointed out the need for land for 200,000 houses around London, in addition to those being provided inside the conurbation and in new expanded towns. Schemes were drawn up for using the Lea valley and some derelict railway sites. The emphasis shifted from the idea of checking the spatial growth of London to that of the provision of amenity and areas of high landscape and agricultural value. The green belt contained many non-conformable, but permitted activities – schools, hospitals and cemeteries, and some of which were inappropriate, but seemingly unavoidable, such as gravel diggings, sewage works etc. With these and the existence of tongues of urbanized land stretching far beyond London along lines of communication, the green belt in places well merited one complainant's description of it as 'a ditch between two sub-topias'. However, extensions (in 1971 almost all of unbuilt-up Hertfordshire was added) have meant that in the future much more of the 'green belt' will be truly green. Roughly one tenth, in fact, of the land surface of England and Wales is now designated as proposed green belt. As D. Thomas remarks,[27] this large proportion of the total can only be justified if the motives behind its preservation are beyond question. Green belts have tended from time to time to become weapons in the battle between counties and neighbouring cities and between the 'haves' and the 'have nots'. In the recent massive study by Peter Hall *et al.*[28] the conclusion is reached that the containment policy, by rendering the most needed building land unavailable, has helped to push up land prices right through the system and moreover has increased the segregation of two housing classes, the owner/occupier and the council tenant.

Certainly, if the green belt was intended to restrict the growth of cities it has both succeeded and failed. 'Restricting city growth' by green belts is a concept which only makes sense in terms of rounding off the blobs on the map. What has happened in reality is that the city has incorporated its countryside as a new kind of park, then simply stepped over the girdle and continued its growth beyond. In the case of London, this 'ripple' effect of urban development is now such that even the outer metropolitan area has shown signs of loss of population to even more distant areas such as East Anglia.

Mounting public unease about city growth in the 1930s led the Royal Commission on the Distribution of Industrial Population (appointed in 1937) to call for a national authority to consider 'the methods by which such decentralisation, or dispersal, should be encouraged and secured, in the form of garden cities or garden suburbs, satellite towns, trading estates, or by the development of existing small towns or regional centres'.[29] The Abercromby plan provided for the dispersal of 1¾ million from the built-up central area of London, including the now highly conservative total of 400,000 to be housed in 8 new satellite towns beyond the green belt.

The story of the new towns and cities is relatively so well known that it has obscured the greater, though more fragmented, role of the private builder in catering for, and to a degree helping to foster, a desire to live beyond the conurbation boundary. Between 1951 and 1971 the new towns represented only 18 % of the population growth of south-east England outside the metropolitan area. Two thirds of all houses built in the south-east outside Greater London since 1955 have been built by the private sector. The 'natural' growth of existing settlements, to which the private, speculative builder is the greatest contributor, is expected to accommodate 70 % of the total population increase in the south-east up to 1981, while even in the new and expanded towns, private development will be responsible for a great deal of the housing provision. A significant proportion of this represents demand for dwellings by people working in London, and using the public transport network to get there. The large, London based, private developer, using large sites bought at relatively low prices in the outer 'country' ring beyond the green belt, plays almost as significant a role in urban colonization as Dyos's Victorian spec. builders once did.[30] We need to understand this world no less than that of public authority planning. After all, according to one report, 18 millionaires were created in the house-building industry in 16 months up to October 1972, a time of hitherto unprecedented rises in house prices. A large building firm like Wimpey or Wates is, looking at it broadly, as much a 'public enterprise' as any big city housing department. It is aided by, and dependent for its operations on, a vast network of planning regulations, public services, growth strategies, incentives to potential customers, as well as government financial policy. As Hall's important study suggests, it is housing policies rather than planning policies that have been responsible for the greatest ills of urban development since the war.

There is what Pahl has called[31] 'a dispersed city' in the country around London, based upon the availability to many people of a high degree of personal mobility and consequently the potential of a highly dispersed activity pattern. Motorization for the millions, comments Maurice Ash,[32] changed London, not the Abercromby plan. It is possible to live up to 50 miles from one's place of work, and to conduct a wide range of social activities in a similar diversity of places. As in the Victorian era, but on a greatly extended geographical plane, availability and cost of housing and transport open up a wide range of opportunities and constraints for individuals. For many, notably the more privileged, the real resultant habitat is as much the region as a whole as it is one particular locality. Stockbrokers commuting to London from the Surrey hills might be in the country, but they are certainly not of it. They are, in fact, dispersed Londoners, however much anti-urban romanticism may cause them to repudiate the label. In fact, two thirds of stockbrokers live in the villages and smallish towns of 'rural' south-east England, while in the same area very substantial farming operations are carried on by managerial and professional people working part-time. A countryside full of highly mobile people, not greatly attached to specific 'places' is, in an important sense, an urban countryside. 'Thus, when the middle class extends itself from the city into the region, then, in this respect, the city has extended itself into the metropolitan region.'[33]

The logic of the development of the south-east as 'dispersed London' has now been accepted, in the Strategic Plan for the south-east, which envisages the area as a matrix of interlinked but individually viable urban settlements, with a transport system which cuts across the spokes of the wheel. As Ash points out, the GLC motorway box was, against this, a conservative project, designed to enhance the centre and make it attractive to the car-user and the affluent. Once again, the character of the transport network is seen as central to urban form, but more importantly to the relationships in the city between those with and those without power or privilege (a point made by Engels over a century before).

One of the most important impacts of the growth of the dispersed city is upon the population, resources and needs of the old core cities. The populations of the largest cities are now in decline.

Greater London lost 6·8 % of its population between 1961 and 1971; this masks the true situation of the inner boroughs, where, for example, Islington lost 22·7 % and Tower Hamlets 19·4 %. Between 1951 and 1971, again, the population of the city of Liverpool went down by almost 25 % from almost 800,000 to about 600,000 and the tendency towards the latter part of the period was for this exodus to accelerate. In one year alone, 1971–2, the loss was 14,700.

Now this loss of population, for which both private and commercial decisions and public policies are responsible, leaves the core city with an increasing proportion of its citizens in need of public help but with a diminishing resource-base from which to provide it. Take, for example, the case of Liverpool. In the 1960s, three new towns in its hinterland, Skelmersdale, Runcorn and Warrington, were planned to take 160,000 from inner Merseyside. By 1971 most of this impact was still to be felt. Hence, not only were the owner/occupiers, with their rateable values and their spending power, increasingly not living in the core city, but so also were the skilled manual workers in public authority housing, leaving behind a much higher proportion of the unskilled and semi-skilled in the core city. The 1966 census showed that while 8·1 % of the workforce (England and Wales) were unskilled manual workers, these were only 5·3 % of the workforce of the new towns but 10·3 % of that of the large cities. Again, since it is largely the young who migrate to the new towns and private housing developments, the population left behind also tends to rise in average age and the proportion of the elderly to increase. In 1951, 13·1 % of the citizens of Liverpool were over 60; in 1971 the proportion was 18·5 %. The much higher proportions of the semi-skilled and unskilled and the elderly in the old core cities means that there is a much higher than average share of needs for services but a lower overall rateable value with which to meet these responsibilities. Liverpool's rateable yield rose in the 1950s and 1960s by only half of the national average. The government's rate support grant has been the device which, theoretically, should have equalized the load as between local authorities – for instance, between core cities and surrounding areas. But the needs element in the grant has been tied chiefly to population and the number of school children. Hence a city whose population is in steep decline does not necessarily have its real needs met, and central government help may actually be falling.

Naturally, up to 20 % of a core city's population cannot drain off without great effects on the remainder. Not only can it have great effects on the resultant assessment of needs and resources given the methods hitherto used in Britain, but it can hardly not have malign social effects on the specific areas of greatest exported population. It is the inner third of the core city which is affected, not the outer, more prosperous two thirds.

The inner area of Liverpool in fact, is 'going to look very sick' as the city's chief planning officer has put it.[34] While the demolition of unfit houses advances and net population slumps, the net result for a considerable time is less that of substantially improved housing conditions for those left behind, than a continuance of their existing situation while large tracts of emptied land lie derelict, waiting on the movement of men and machinery.

London, as we have seen, is peculiar, the problems of its poorest citizens endless. For in addition to problems similar to those just outlined, the associated effects of government economic policies, planning policies, the growth of the 'service' sector and the particular commercial forces concentrated there, have been to create in London, and particularly in inner London, pressures not, on the whole, to be found elsewhere. There is a high concentration of activities in the service sector, such as transport, hotels and restaurants etc., paying comparatively low wages; at the same time, the effects of inflation are more marked than elsewhere, and have added to existing pressures in the property and housing fields, thus reducing still further the purchasing power of many not only on low but often on what would elsewhere be seen as middle incomes. A high proportion of those most under pressure are employed in the public sector and are hence directly affected by government efforts at income restraint. As a result inner London's transport suffers from endemic understaffing, its schooling system from high turnover and discontent on the part of teachers, and its housing is woefully incapable of meeting the needs of the workers on whose services the life of the city depends.

The dispersal of the city, therefore, is a process which involves, as it has always done, questions of poverty and power and privilege. In this century it has increasingly concerned public policy, whether exercised at the national or the local level. Although it is in the south-east that the trend is most fully developed, this transformation of the city is a general phenomenon. Indeed, the extension of 'built-up' areas has been greatest, since 1960, in the north-west, not the south-east, owing to the dispersal of hitherto very high densities; and this despite absolute decreases in population in much of the former area (which demonstrates, if it were needed, that it is living standards rather than population as such which create pressure on land).

And how far can the tendency go? As far as rendering the distinction between 'the city' and 'the country' meaningless. Research had suggested, says Derek Senior,[35] 'that the last surviving patch of the English heartland to remain untouched by the emergence of the city region as its dominant social form', was the north Cotswold area. By the 1960s, however, it appeared that even here there were now more commuters than agricultural workers. From the heart of the most depopulated part of this district, the parish of Blockley (Gloucestershire) alone was sending three coach-loads of women daily to work in the needlemaking industry of Redditch, 22 miles away as the crow flies.

Thus does the 'core and centre of the English world; mid-most England, unmitigated England',[36] move to a new rhythm.

Chapter 2 Where We are Now: Interpretations

That was a way of putting it; factually, a little breathlessly. But without, perhaps, much reflection on the meaning. That, especially in Britain, is the most difficult part.

For such an urbanized society the British contribution to the store of ideas about 'the city' has been fairly modest. Students of urban politics and sociology are still quite likely to learn as much about Chicago or suburban America as about Birmingham or Surrey. The number of good books dealing with the government and politics of British cities, taken together, could be counted almost on the fingers of one hand. Powerful and long-standing as the tradition of British historical scholarship is, there has been, until very recently, rather little attention given to the development of the cities since the industrial revolution. The appearance in 1974 of the massive two-volume collection of essays edited by Professor Dyos on the Victorian city[1] may signify that at last this strange neglect is at an end.

Perhaps the reason why we know so little about our cities is because for a long time they were not accepted. British anti-urbanism has a lengthy history. From the peace of Hampshire, Jane Austen even thought there was 'something direful' in the sound, 'Birmingham'. The classes whose wealth the industrial revolution created aimed to join the landed aristocracy, or at least acquire a country house, the widely acknowledged symbol of success. One writer noted in 1885 that 'the possession of land is the guarantee of respectability, and the love of respectability and land is inveterate in our race'.[2] Many who could not hope for that could still hope to retreat from the city proper to the stronghold of a suburban villa. And, of course, flight from the towns for those who could, was highly valid on health grounds. A potent mood amongst the intelligentsia of the Victorian age was revulsion against ugly economics and ugly places. Many of the 'educated' had a conservative fear of 'mass society' – that the cities harboured a threat to order, deference and hierarchy, whether it came from trade and capital or from 'the mob'. On the other side, William Morris's socialism was trenchantly anti-urban. The British brand of anti-city feelings, largely upper and middle class in tone, had its counterpart in the much more 'democratic' ideological climate of America. There the idea of cities as distasteful, corrupting, un-American, has been voiced in one form or another in every generation since Thoreau. The wilderness has been a compelling symbol of purity. In both countries, the pre-industrial settlement, such as the English village, or the New England colonial town, has been idealized, while the image of the tight communal life of the 'market-place within a wall' of the European medieval cities still gives rise to various forms of pseudo-medievalism in Britain, particularly on civic occasions.

Not that this anti-urban climate has been entirely un-progressive' in its results. From the late nineteenth century Britain has had a strong town and country planning movement, and we are all the beneficiaries of its achievements. It was much concerned with the preservation of the countryside and with the generation of ideas about the nature of future urban development (which was largely seen as a matter of restoring urban man to nature). In terms of what it set out to do, it was rather successful, with the garden cities, new towns, green belts and national parks to its credit. For all its progressivism, however, it was an essentially reactionary movement, in the sense that it aimed at containing the city and preserving the countryside from contamination by it. Comparatively little attention or mental energy was devoted to the life of the existing large cities themselves. It may be that, fundamentally, these liberals and idealists had given up the large industrial cities as irredeemable. Certainly, the green and pleasant shires were more promising places to build Jerusalem than among the dark satanic mills of the industrial cities. In any event, while a tradition of imaginative thinking about the future of town and country grew up in Britain, the recoil against the big cities meant that precious little in the way of creative concern was expended on *them*, who needed it most.

One place, for example, where British writers, both liberal and conservative, mingled entirely praiseworthy concern for the quality of the environment with a crude revulsion against the city, was the book of essays *Britain and the Beast* (1938) edited by Clough Williams-Ellis.[3] The theme is the despoliation of the countryside by urbanization, mass leisure, private vulgarity, governmental boorishness and virtually every other conceivable destroyer of rural peace and beauty. The essayists are full of lyrical tenderness over the lesser celandine, the English lane and Binsey poplars. Their concern was legitimate, and thankfully it was shortly to bear some fruit in post-war counter-measures such as the National Parks Act. And their battle is a continuing one. It would, however, have done the essayists in this volume, and their ideal, more credit had many of them not shown indifference, and in some cases, a scarcely veiled hostility, to both cities and city people for what 'they' were doing to Britain. Now the rape of things that are old and green and of the earth is indeed heartbreaking, wherever it occurs; but it was not the greatest beastliness in Britain in the 1930s, nor is it now.

This tradition of distaste for the contemporary city has been added to by a strong strain of criticism coming from sociologists concerned with the condition of man in an urban setting. The founding fathers of sociology, and especially Weber, Durkheim and Simmel, were much concerned with the human costs accompanying urbanization. Generally, they saw the division of labour characteristic of city life requiring people to behave towards each other in terms dictated by their socio-economic functions, as employers, employees, producers, consumers. The effective, expressive, dimensions of life were perforce segregated out into segments and men lost a sense of 'the whole'. The process of encountering urbanization was seen as accompanying the withering away of man's inherited traditional beliefs and mythologies, tribal and kinship attachments. Faced with a novel variety of contacts and behavioural choices, he was left at

33

best, vulnerable, because alone and without a structured setting for his life. The early sociologists were much more conceptually rich than this, of course, but in crude terms, these ideas to which they gave form have become widely disseminated and often accepted. It can amply be demonstrated that this syndrome of views posits too sharp a break between social experience in urban and pre-urban society and it ignores the extent to which the city contains countervailing social networks – the street and neighbourhood, church, trade union, political party, club, etc. If city life can be difficult for those not provided with a secure structure for living within, so too life can be difficult, if not impossible, for those whom non-urban communities choose to define as non-conformers. But what matters is not the truth of the picture of desensitized and demoralized urban man, but its power as an image. There can be little doubt of its widespread appeal.

These several traditions and attitudes add up, in consequence, to a formidable amalgam of ignorance and despair about the city – hardly a helpful climate for the generation of ideas and action.

Hard on the heels of the 'city as instrument of decline and fall' school have come those who, observing late twentieth-century technological society, feel the city itself is now withering away in any case. Kenneth E. Boulding, for example, argues that in so far as the city has been *the* artifact of civilization, its passing away is now taking place because science has created 'post-civilization'.[4] Certainly it is true that many of the factors which gave rise to the growth of cities as we have hitherto thought of them, now work towards their dispersal. This raises, of course, a question of definition.

According to Max Weber, the 'urban community' in its 'pure' or 'ideal' form was defined essentially by its consisting of a market and a fortification; it also had its own court and at least partially autonomous law-making, with at least partial autonomy in the choice of the governors by the burghers. One by one the bulk of these distinguishing characteristics has thinned in meaning until they have disappeared or assumed a purely symbolic form. The fortification has long been that of the nation, more recently of the international bloc. Militarily, far from being a defensive unit the city is now highly vulnerable, to attack both from abroad and from guerrilla activity internally. The markets of modern society are national and international. The market place can be anywhere – or nowhere, thanks to post and telephone. Many European medieval cities had substantial degrees of legal autonomy, the law being made in each place according to its own customs and ruling families. Now, within one country, or at least within one unit of a federation, the law itself does not vary and any variations in legal application probably have little if anything to do with place as such. A degree of distinctiveness was lent to cities by the entrepreneurs who built them up and governed them in former times. But while an old established business élite based upon old prestige firms may continue to exist, its impact on the life of most cities is fairly slight, confined perhaps to a shadowy role as a kind of social establishment, well represented on the committees of the higher prestige charities. Every city centre bears witness to the tendency of modern commercial activity to diminish local uniqueness.

Of all Weber's characteristics of 'the city', local self-government has enjoyed the fullest survival into today and would seem to be the only one certain of a future. It has become commonplace to regard the political autonomy of local governments as an empty shell. In this aspect yet again, some would argue, successive developments over the last century, while progressively increasing the burden city government is called upon to bear, have steadily whittled away the autonomy of local representatives and administrators to the level where many people in Britain see them as expressing their freedom of action merely in the interpretation of what has been laid down nationally. Emphasis on this trend, however, has led people to fail to appreciate the freedoms which local governments *do* exercise (not always, perhaps, well understood by themselves) and of the wide variations in practice which witness to these freedoms. In recent years in the fields of planning and education alone, British city governments have revealed a vigour in pursuing individual policies which belies the argument that they are mere puppets on the central government string.

Much indeed, of the very great confusion of thought attending British local government reform in the mid twentieth century has arisen from the fact that the idea of the city as a governmental unit has retained its power while many of the other dimensions which went to make up the traditional concept of the city have altered, or even disappeared. Awareness of this change, the abundant evidence that we are not where we were, was enough to fuel the movement to transform the governmental scene at sub-national level. The proposals and the changes, however, reflected rather than clarified the great confusion as to where we are now, and where we might be going.

Our stock of ideas about what 'cities' are comes largely from a time when ways of life and the social relations engendered in the 'city' were distinct from those of 'the country', as different as Dickens's London was from Hardy's reconstruction of mid-Victorian Dorset.[5] How much would that difference amount to now? It would be foolish to say it was negligible. Space, density and access remain. But overwhelmingly the two are subject to conditions which operate on a national, not a local, basis. Consider the difference between town and country now, and a century ago, with regard to communication and popular culture. Or the determination and distribution of power and poverty. If there are problems that are distinctive to London rather than to Dorset, these are more meaningfully seen as national problems which happen to have their setting in a densely rather than a lightly populated area. From the sociologist's point of view, as R. E. Pahl puts it, 'the social processes which create urban ways of life relate to the whole society'.[6] The study of the city is the study of society.

The city, then, in its ideal form as Weber discussed it is largely dead. We cannot return to it any more than a man can return to his own infancy, but we must explore the question of what it is becoming if we are to retain the capacity to make our future history. When we talk about the urbanization of our society we are talking about a development so comparatively recent and so complex in character that it would be crassly presumptuous to assume we have yet done more than begin to understand its full impact upon us. C. A. Doxiadis,[7] who has virtually created his own science of human settlements, notes that only in the last 10,000 years (i.e. within the last 0·5 % of man's life span on earth), have men been living in permanent settlements. Only within the last 6,000 years have men lived in recognizable cities. In turn for most of this period cities have been static settlements in which the balance of population, technology and the land was relatively unchanging.

The point is worth making, because it is hard to consider the modern city except in terms of dynamic growth. In 1800 there were 21 European cities with populations of over 100,000, holding a thirty-fifth of Europe's population. A century later, in 1900, there were 147 such cities in Europe and, with 40 million, they now held a tenth of Europe's population. It is estimated[8] that in world terms, as late as 1800 only 3 % of a world population of 906 million lived in centres (750 in all) of 5,000 inhabitants or more. A larger proportion of the vastly increased world population of 1950 lived in 'settlements' with populations of over one million than in 1800 had lived in *all* settlements of 5,000 or over. In Britain, 77 % of the population lives in urban areas of 5,000 or more, while well over a third of the Dutch people now live in Randstad, the ring-shaped agglomeration which links together the cities of Amsterdam, The Hague and Rotterdam. We have little reason to believe that this phenomenon of growth will do anything other than continue, whatever the form it may take, for it is not fuelled by population increase alone, but by a considerable complex of forces.

Doxiadis argues that one can trace a progressive growth in the size and complexity of human settlements through 12 stages, beginning at the 'dwelling group' of perhaps 40 people (such as survived until well into this century in rural Wales and Ireland) through the neighbourhood and small town to the metropolis and conurbation. Beyond the latter stage comes the point where a series of conurbations and large cities have grown so near to merging into one another as to form a conurbation of conurbations, a loosely linked, nearly continuous band of recognizably non-rural settlement. Patrick Geddes saw this development coming, over half a century ago. He saw London as 'a house province spreading over, absorbing, a great part of South East England',[9] and, he wrote, 'The expectation is not absurd that the not very distant future will see practically one vast city-line along the Atlantic coast [of the USA] for 500 miles.'[10] An interlocking urban belt now does stretch for 500 miles from southern Maine to Virginia, south of Washington. Similar interlocking belts in the making of North America include southern California and the area round the Great Lakes. The latter's eastern extremity, the region near Buffalo, NY, is itself linked by strong communications lines with the western edge of the Atlantic belt. This phenomenon has been called 'megalopolis'. There is no ultimate end to this process, argues Doxiadis, short of world-city, or ecumenopolis. This is not to say there will not be vast tracts of desert and wilderness and land reserved for recreation and for agriculture. But it will have been so reserved as a conscious act of policy, or because it is unsuitable territory for urbanized settlement. In ecumenopolis, the entire surface of the world will have become recognizably the dwelling place of urbanized humanity, says Doxiadis.

Lewis Mumford[11] expresses his, and many people's, horror at the apparent easy acceptance of such a situation ('an urbanoid nonentity') and argues that to restrict the growth of population is better than to 'plan for urbanizing every possible acre of the planet'. But Doxiadis argues that the restriction of world population is not likely to take place (if at all) on a scale sufficiently great to affect his overall thesis. Increased private affluence even in a static population leads to greatly increased pressures on space. Add to that the acceptance of public responsibility for providing decent living space for all, and there is agenda enough for future urban growth, whatever the trend of population.

In Britain we have already seen, as Geddes predicted, the Londonization of a great part of southern England; while there have been agreements for the export of London population not only into this area but to places as far removed as Burnley, Lancs, the south-west, and deepest East Anglia. Lloyd Rodwin argues that we have been witnessing the transformation of the whole country into 'for all practical purposes a linear megalopolitan complex with London, the central metropolitan city, closely linked to Birmingham, Liverpool, Manchester and Glasgow', with a fringe of 'extensive green-belt zones reserved for agriculture, recreation and other rural and leisure purpose activities' and with, between the urban areas, a number of 'key satellites threaded together along high speed transportation corridors'.[12] Certainly the 1960s alone saw British Rail priding itself on 'moving' the north nearer to the Midlands (and the high speed passenger train is likely to be one of the most important transport developments of the next 30 years), the opening of a motorway or near motorway standard road link from London, through the west Midlands and south Lancashire to Glasgow, and, significantly, the conception of plans for two major new cities (Milton Keynes and Preston/ Chorley) both astride these major road and rail arteries. Contrast the growth, vigour and attraction of this central spine with the difficulty of travelling *across* it between places on its periphery (say, from Shrewsbury to Cambridge) and the relative torpor of regions out on limbs not strongly related to it (such as, say, West Cumberland or much of Wales). If since 1945 a policy of 'letting rip' had been adopted, with no planning and no development area policy, this tendency would have become much stronger, and the central spine of England *would* have, by now, largely become filled with what Melvin Webber calls 'undifferentiated urban space'.

Is there, then, an English megalopolis? By American standards, not quite. Thanks to planning legislation, one recent important study argues, megalopolis has been 'denied'.[13] In any case, students in the USA have recently been inclined to regard the case for the existence of a megalopolis on the east coast as overstated. But, of course, the great northern industrial cities of England are dispersing population and, thanks to improved transport, coming closer together. And this region where so many of the beginnings of the industrial/urban 'revolution' took place *can* be seen as one end of a great western European belt of near-continuous urban development, encompassing the Midlands, south-east England, the river/port cities of Germany and the low countries, and the great Rhine–Ruhr/Lorraine industrial area, and closely linked to separated centres round Paris and northern Italy. But to see this as a coming megalopolis may be merely to put a label on the obvious, pretentiously. What has happened, in effect, is that the areas large in population and activity in 1900 have grown larger (the south-east's population grew by 70 % from 1900 to 1966, the west Midlands' by 65 %), and have attracted to them and the areas between them a great deal of what there has been in the way of new development and growth generating activity. It would be better to characterize what is emerging as a series of city regions with strong interlinking arteries.

The capacity to add new to old work to which Jane Jacobs draws attention as vital to the economy of cities[14] has tended to increase the pull of capital cities like London and Paris, and that of centres of industries needing a large range of diverse components, such as, classically, the car industry. These push the built-up frontier forward in fringe suburbs and satellite towns. Another important element in this tendency has been provided by the great growth in recent years of service and white-collar jobs. In England and Wales the number of office workers increased by 41 % between 1951 and 1961 as against a general increase in occupations of 8 %. And the larger the centre, the larger was this increase in service and white-collar jobs, especially of course in the London region where half the office space newly built in England and Wales has been located.[15]

If England and Wales *as a whole* are compared with America's north-eastern seaboard 'megalopolis', the similarities in several key respects – area, population, density, proportion of developed land, are striking.[16] Put in another way, Patmore estimates that half of England is taken up by the 'living space' zones of existing urban centres of over 30,000 people.[17]

The country is not, despite alarms occasionally raised in the south-east, on the verge of disappearing under a vast concrete jungle. Indeed, studies have indicated that only 10·8 % of the land surface of England and Wales is 'urban' (though this is double what it was in 1900) and by the turn of the century this will only rise at most to about 15 %, despite the maturation of building projects of giant size.[18] Even the train traveller between Liverpool and Manchester can (just about) see more of green fields than of anything else. The sheer expanse of concrete and brick is not the point; rather it is the dominance of 'urbanism' over the culture, the modes of life of almost all of the people, and penetrating its physical presence into tracts of territory geographically far removed from the 'cities' proper. In one Lleyn peninsula parish, 36 % of the ratepayers are second home owners, most, one presumes, from the big English cities.[19] Only 43,000 people live in the Lake District, but upwards of 20 million now live within 3 hours' driving distance. It could be argued that the chief purpose of the Lake District is to be for these millions as much a part of their urban living-space as the municipal park was to the urbanite of an earlier generation (and still is, of course).

It is proper that such areas should be cherished to be places of renewal for urban man. (The difficulty is that intensive use erodes the very antithesis between rural/natural and urban/fabricated which makes a national park *different* from a municipal park. Cynically, one might suggest that anyone with a care for the wildernesses, for the high and lonely places of the earth, might fruitfully endeavour to *prevent* them from being designated national parks.) In any event, the implication of all this, as Cullingworth[20] urges, is that planning in Britain has to be on a national scale, for, in effect, no part of the country is now immune from the pressures and conflicts of value that our urban/industrial revolution has produced. The city and society have become one, and the land its living-space.

Lewis Mumford expresses strong dissent from Doxiadis's

41

urgings that we should accept 'megalopolis' as a 'given', and work from there. All the more notable, then, that there should be such striking agreement between them on one point – that in the development and renewal of cities a central role must be reserved for the internal 'community' or neighbourhood cell. Ebenezer Howard's ideal of a modest sized town of 30,000 built up of a hierarchy of cells of around 5,000 each, Mumford suggests, is the ideal basis for a network of neighbourhood organizations, though in the largest cities of all, such as New York, he proposes 100,000. This, because the dynamism of urban growth must be, not channelled into acceptable paths, but conquered and tamed. 'The forces' he writes, 'that have formed our cities in the past are now almost automatically, by their insensate dynamism, wrecking them and threatening to destroy whole countries and continents.'[21] Mumford wants to rebuild the city from the ground up, by giving special encouragement to the formative, stabilizing, order-making forces, in the hope that they may control the destructive dynamism. To Mumford, the neighbourhood is good because it is the primary locus not merely of social life but of moral behaviour; while within eutopia, Doxiadis's word for the city created by, acceptable to, both the scientist and the dreamer, the dynamic city would consist of static cells, each a small human community. 'It is within such static cells that we can save man from the city that will crush him; it is within them that the community can have complete freedom for its expressions, and man for his life.'[22] Here, Doxiadis is thinking of the cell in terms of its built form. 'Someday, if people should bring their cars into the human part of such a community, we will laugh at them, as we do now at people who have entered a drawing-room wearing their muddy boots.'[23]

To Doxiadis, eutopia entails human communities of around 9,000 people. The idea of creating such a cellular structure within the larger body of the city, city region, megalopolis or whatever, has important implications for the structure of government in cities. It begs many questions, about, for example, the concept of a 'community' based on a given territory of a city, and much thinking by architects and planners along these lines has been sociologically naive. There are many more difficulties than are often acknowledged, in finding appropriate territories and appropriate levels of responsibility within which to relate the city as a governmental construct to whatever it has become as a social and economic one. Nevertheless Doxiadis is surely right to discern, whether we accept his conclusions or not, that the problem of the future organization of an urban world is a question also of the future organization of democratic politics and government.

In such an eutopia the best type of democracy can operate, the one which guarantees the optimum of freedoms at all levels, by easily centralising decisions where necessary, but leaving all other decisions at the lowest possible level in every occasion where the personal contact between people is easier; and thus the operation of society is based on better understanding of its needs.[24]

Chapter 3 Keeping the System Going: the Ethos of Urban Government

As we have seen, the dimension of the city's existence which retains the most distinct identity is that relating to its function as a unit of government. Like any long-standing social activity, city government in Britain has evolved particular traditions, or styles of approach to its tasks, and has attracted to its service particular types of people; and it has worked within particular legal and resource frameworks laid down by central government.

It is only very recently that the government and politics of cities has begun to emerge from long neglect by students, and there is still some way to go before we fill in the evidence on how the system works, beyond, that is, the purely formal level of descriptions of constitutional powers. Until recent years there was no really comprehensive scrutiny of the objectives, structure and operational assumptions of local government since the system was set up deep in the Victorian era.

The ethos of our present system is the product of a slow, undramatic evolution over nearly a century. Its basic constitutional framework, the norms and values by which it is conducted were established in another age, and change in them is a far more subtle process than one of simply reforming the structure. A backward glance at the course of evolution which has brought us to where we are now may help to illustrate this; and to make the point that while some of the problems and complaints surrounding local government are unique to the conditions of current city life, some are perennial.

Defining urban areas for the purposes of local government means recognizing boundaries between different jurisdictions. For the Victorians this presented fewer problems than today. It was largely self-evident where a city began and ended. There were occasional disputes between contiguous towns, such as Liverpool's attempted take-over of Bootle (resulting in failure and the raising of flags for 'independence day' in the latter), but these were not of central importance. Towns could be defined by their continuous built-up areas, and periodically, if belatedly, their boundaries were adjusted to take account of extensions in area. The 1888 Local Government Act established the county borough system with 61 county boroughs for the larger towns and cities, plus the County of London. From then down to the 1920s there were frequent new grantings of county borough status (21 in all) and extensions of existing county boroughs (250,000 acres in 109 separate actions). Two thirds of all requests for changes or new boundaries were granted. Thus down to the 1920s it could be said that the cities as local government units more or less kept pace with changes in the location of population.

From the 1926 Local Government Act until today, however, this has not been the case. The Act, the result of pressure from the county councils, largely curtailed the encroachment of county boroughs on the neighbouring counties, while the pro-longed period of governmental rethinking of the local boundary problem since the war largely had the same immobilizing effect. The one major departure since the war, the creation of the Greater London Council in 1963, was (with the exception of the creation of Teesside CB) the last attempt to express the city, for governmental purposes, in terms of continuous built-up areas. One of the immediate precipitators of the setting up of the Redcliffe-Maud Commission on reform was, indeed, that the attempt of the commission on English local government boundaries (under the 1958 Act) to induce some rationalization had proved slow and painfully difficult, largely due to powerful local resistance to change. But also, in any case, by this time, to define the city on the crudest possible outward visible evidence was plainly to adhere to an obsolete concept. This *might* have continued validity as an administratively convenient unit, since the line has to be drawn somewhere; but it would have to take its chance with other concepts of the city. In the event, the Redcliffe-Maud commissioners found the idea of the city as an urban island in a rural sea to be a fatal defect of the local government system of contemporary Britain. Town and country, they accepted, were interdependent. Sadly, however, their recommendations were not based upon any consistent theory as to how this interdependence worked or might relate to the tasks local government has to perform. Hence many of their authorities would have had boundaries at least as irrational as the old ones. Following the Conservative Local Government Act of 1972 a different, but equally incoherent, set of boundaries was devised and the new system put into effect. Derek Senior's minority report,[1] advocating a system based on the recognition of the city region as the form of urban settlement having most reality and viability today, shows that a rational scheme could, given the necessary research effort, have been devised.

Important as area might be, however, it is not as important as power. In fact, although conventional wisdom has long had it that size and efficiency go together, most evidence, including that produced by the research for the Redcliffe-Maud Commission, suggests that this is not so. Regardless of size, what matters is what goes on within the given urban government. How, then, has its ethos been built up?

The mid years of the nineteenth century, from the Municipal Corporations Act (1835) to the Local Government Act of 1888, were years in which a complicated, venerable but often inept and corrupt system of town government by oligarchy was replaced by a system which, being elective, could to that extent be termed 'democratic'. In fact it was so in only a limited sense. Government by an unrepresentative oligarchy of the wealthiest burgesses, responsible to few but themselves, was replaced by government by a body of men elected by a progressively widening franchise and responsible to their electorate. Sometimes this resulted in a wider mix of social classes being represented on the council, and sometimes it didn't. Foster has shown that in

Oldham until 1865 all the mayors of the town were drawn from the 70 capitalist families whom he has detected; only when these moved out to pleasanter pastures was there opportunity for the mayoralty to open up to a wider populace.[2]

From the mid nineteenth century, as Hennock has shown,[3] it was widely complained that the replacement of substantial and respectable men by others lower down the social scale had taken place. From then on, he illustrates, complaint about the calibre of local government representatives was 'code' for complaint about the absence of men of high occupational status. Of course what matters here is really what the representative is *for*. When the corporation becomes a great undertaking on the scale of a large business, then the skills appropriate to running it might be akin to those of successful businessmen. On the other hand, if it is a big spender of ratepayers money, then the prudential ethos of the small businessmen and 'shopocracy' naturally comes into play. Later, when the council becomes a large employer of labour, one rationale for the intrusion of working men on to the council is to speak for its employees. Hennock shows how all of these considerations are relevant in considering the composition and activity of Victorian city councils.

Today, factors like these have substantially lessened salience in the face of the two vastly important developments – the great increase in the sheer scope of local government's impact on the life of every citizen, and the great growth in the dependence of local government on its administrative machine, its own professionals and bureaucrats. In this context, what the modern urban government needs, arguably, is effective representatives of citizen interests at least as much as effective makers of policy. And it needs more open government, in which it is a natural stance for the council to be sensitive to the citizens' definition of the situation. Here, the evidence of our historical inheritance is discouraging.

It is a commonplace that few people today can be got to take much interest in their local government. But it is less often understood perhaps, that this is *not* the end product of a

lengthy process of decline. Whatever its causes, this apathy
suits well a system devised in a world in which it was assumed
by all those who mattered, that government was government of
the grateful many, by the few. As George Jones amply demonstrates in his study of the history of Wolverhampton council,
many of the lamentations made about local government are
perennial. An alderman in 1897 'had to lament that so many of
our leading townsmen refused to take their part in the government of the town to which they belonged'.[4] Turnout at elections
in Wolverhampton in the 1890s was high – 65 % to 75 % – but
in most years only one or two wards faced contests, and in 1897
only 15 % of the town's population was eligible to vote in any
case. Jones argues cogently that popular participation in local
politics is considerably *greater* today than it was in the 1890s.
'More people', he says, 'vote, stand for and are elected to the
council now than before the days of party, and they come from
a wider range of occupations.'[5]

Nevertheless, Jones acknowledges, the handful of individuals
who played leading roles in town government have always been:

a very small proportion of the town's population. The majority have no
continuing and deep interest in local government . . . In all about nine
hundred at most out of a population of 150,000 had an active interest in
local politics, and that is a generous estimate. Very few people keep the
system going.[6]

A glance at the occupational composition of city councils
illustrates that during the years when the traditions of contemporary local government were being fashioned, the vast
majority of the social groups in the population were not
represented. In Wolverhampton in the years 1888 to 1890, as
many as 33 % of council members were owners or controllers of
substantial manufacturing enterprises, while manufacturers
along with 'professionals' and shopkeepers made up 72 % of
the total. Only 6 % were 'workers'. Few workmen would have had
time for council activity even if other opportunities such as
access through either of the political parties had been open.
Chamberlain's 'Birmingham school' believed in recruitment of

men of a wide range of classes. Nevertheless, in the 1880s and 90s 40 % of Birmingham council were 'professionals' and owners of large businesses. We must be warned, however, against too easy generalization; in Leeds at the same period the dominant interest was that of the small businessmen and shopkeepers.[7] In Liverpool, in the late Victorian years and the early years of this century, some semblance of popular participation in affairs was given by the 'Orange democracy', as it were, of the Conservative Workingmen's Association, but this was a deviant case and had more to do with the building of an electoral machine on an 'ethnic' base than anything else. Whatever the differences between cities, none of them could be claimed, by any stretch of the imagination, to be models of open participatory democracy.

In these 'early modern' city governments, the ethos of public service was strong, but paternalistic. Asa Briggs gives, for example, the case of the domination of Middlesbrough by Henry Bolckow and the connection of the Pease family. 'Bolckow', said Prince Arthur, opening a park the former had given to Middlesbrough, 'knows what it wants and what its interests are'.[8] (How many council leaders since have prided themselves on that special facility of knowing). In the late nineteenth century the main functions of the council were to provide services to property and to enable trade to flourish. Lighting, paving of streets, provision of tramways, the manufacture of gas and electricity were for 'the good of the town'; they were also, happily, good for business. Moreover, they gave the businessman 'the opportunity to assist the working man far more than could the working man himself'.[9]

As for the electorate, as neither party had a municipal programme or policy, there was little to vote *about*, apart from personalities. P. F. Clarke has remarked of nineteenth-century electoral behaviour in general that what was important was not who one voted *for*, but who one voted *with*.[10] (A view, of course, which retains considerable validity still.)

In time, notably between the wars, the paternalistic, business orientated tradition of leadership began to give way. Local firms became part of national combines. The 75 % derating of industry by the 1929 Local Government Act and the policy of industrial protection in the 1930s all combined to remove incentives to business leaders to participate in local affairs. In addition, room had to be conceded to the representation of working-class and lower middle-class people through the agency of the Labour party. These developments led to the replacement of social leaders by what J. M. Lee has called 'public persons'.[11] But it is open to question whether the basic framework and governmental style changed as much. It remained one in which effective control over administration and policy-making rested in the hands of a relative handful of councillors and aldermen and of a small group of chief officers. In the earlier years the town clerk, often the only person with an overall view of the work of the council, could be, if he chose, the effective leader of the local government, directing its activities, providing an essential push here, frustrating tendencies and initiatives there. Of the key lay leaders, a high proportion were not subject to election at all, because they were aldermen. Most of the faithful, if they remained faithful long enough, could expect, in time, a semi-permanent seat upon the bench. In Wolverhampton the average councillor, in the 1880s as in the 1960s, held his seat for a little over 6 years, while the average alderman in the 1880s held his for 15 years, in the 1960s for over 24 years. Elected councillorship then, as often as not, was merely an apprenticeship or threshold to be crossed on the way to membership of an inner élite of non-representatives holding most of the effective power. Moreover, for what it is worth, there was, over time, little increase in the numbers of elected representatives despite the vast increases in population and in the powers and moneys vested in city councils. In short, more government of more people, but still in the hands of relatively few people.

If the Victorian system was oligarchic, it could at least be argued in mitigation that the sphere of activity widely regarded as appropriate to it was not wide. Up to relatively late in the nineteenth century, much of the day-to-day administration and surveillance was personally conducted by the council members. The sanitary committees in Birmingham and Leeds had the duty of personally inspecting the town for nuisances, and one over-zealous Birmingham councillor actually died in so doing.[12] Parliament in this century has imposed many more duties on local authorities, and shown growing disposition to impose upon them nationwide standards in their administration. Hence the quality of public administration became increasingly important, and so did the role of the administrator.

What has been most notable in this century has been the sheer weight of responsibility undertaken by the relative handful of men who run the cities. For example, planning, and organizing the housing of considerable proportions of the population are responsibilities which did not exist when the 1888 Act was passed. There was no planning legislation, effectively, before 1909. 'Positive' town planning is only a quarter of a century old. It was not until the 1920s and 1930s that city councils began, in a big way, to take responsibility for the provision of mass housing. A measure of the increase in the magnitude of council business is given in Jones's study of Wolverhampton. Between 1900 and 1963 the number of people governed by the council rose from 94,187 to 150,385; the town's rateable value rose from £362,592 to £7,343,693. In 1900 the town raised £79,188 in rates and received £8,994 in government grants. In 1963 the figures were, respectively, £2,844,727 and £2,203,105. At the same time, the number of elected councillors rose by 12.[13]

Despite all this growth in city government, to the point where it looms very large in the lives of the people, the evidence on representation and governmental 'style' would suggest that there have been fewer changes in the relationship between citizens and city government. One of the more important, however, is the incursion of party politics. In the late nineteenth century the parties acted, if at all, simply as electoral mechanisms. They were not concerned with policy-making in the main. In many cases, candidates preferred to eschew parties and political labels altogether, judging them inappropriate in municipal affairs. Bloc voting in the council was similarly undeveloped. The advent of Labour inevitably meant the incursion of 'party politics' and since 1945 this has become the

51

accepted norm. What was new about Labour was that they *had* a municipal policy, and had the practice of holding regular group meetings to concert policy and tactics. Inevitably, the Conservatives had to follow suit, although the Liberals tried to resist the trend. Labour was disposed to operate a group system; it had been part of the trade union tradition in the party; the party found its candidates' running expenses and hence expected in return adherence to a principle of group loyalty. But the group system was also a response to the need to refashion a Victorian tool to do a contemporary job. As Jones puts it, 'the growth in the duties of the council made it vital to have a co-ordinating body to overlook all aspects of the council's work and to harmonise the activities of the various committees'.[14] Whatever the motives of those involved, the growth of party and the caucus in city government was a necessary response to a growing need to agglomerate sufficient power to get things done, and to manage an increasingly wide network of governmental activities. Managerial reform in the 1960s and 70s stems from the same continuing need.

If 'party politics' have been inevitable, not all its effects have been beneficial. The driving of free discussion behind closed doors, while open council became increasingly an inter-party set piece for the apparent benefit of the press, was surely not good for democracy at a time when the impacts of government on the citizen were constantly becoming greater. It would be ironic indeed if one had to conclude that the advent of the Labour party in city politics, far from breaking the tradition of élite domination, had merely substituted a new form of it.

Another important variation upon the 1888 theme has been the changing relationship between the councillor and the paid official. In earlier days, council members and particularly the committee chairmen often had the leisure to devote long hours to their council work, and to become involved in administrative and technical minutiae.[15] As we have seen, many of the leaders were successful businessmen. They were often superior to their chief officers in their knowledge of day-to-day detail. Their social status in the town also helped to maintain, between them and the official, a firmly established employer–employee relationship. All has changed; councillors and perhaps many committee chairmen have neither the time nor the capability to master increasingly complex detail. In their relationship with bureaucrats and experts they are amateurs in a professional world, without even being professionals at politics. In Birmingham, until relatively recently, it has been argued that the survivors of the 'Chamberlain generation' maintained a tight grip on the city's government, and were accustomed to treat their chief officers, however distinguished, as servants. But even there the 'strong council era'[16] ended in the late 1940s and early 1950s when the technical complexities of municipal finance, for example, became really beyond the grasp of many a good businessman. Again, where the odd initiative in town planning in Joseph Chamberlain's time was councillors' work, it became the work of a corps of career planners backed by all the paraphernalia of a profession. The end result, as Jones puts it, describing Wolverhampton, has been that

the work of the committees became more dependent on the expertise of the official, now highly trained, and backed by his professional associations and journals. Also, in 1964, the salaries of the leading officials excepting the Town Clerk were £3,650 a year; much more than that earned by any Labour chairman. In 1900, the chairman was the senior partner; in 1964 the official was the senior partner.[17]

Now, at no time have city governments been given a simple brief to take any action necessary for the welfare of the people. Their job was to administer specific services within parameters laid down elsewhere, each evolving at a different pace from the others. The parameters were in many cases much more permissive of freedom of action than is often thought. But always any action took place within a framework of central government permissions and instructions, with each service developing at different times as needs were newly perceived. This evolution of departmental adminstration of services meant that city problems were defined in departmental/service area terms. Relatively little coordination between departments was called for, while the system could easily lend itself to the opposite – inter-departmental conflicts. City governments were thus geared to defining and acting on their problems *vertically*, as a series of services: education, housing, transport, welfare. A problem that could be isolated in one of these columns could be coped with. But problems like deprivation, one in essence if many sided, have been fragmented into different pieces, each piece appearing in each of the vertical, departmental columns. The administrative machinery, in short, defined the problems in its own image, fragmented and departmentalized. The political parties then often proceeded to compound this process by competing with each other in performing those fragmented tasks. Housing has been a notorious case in particular.

What is worth noticing from this brief glance at 100 years of British city governments? Two things. Firstly, if it is the job of a city's government to cope with a city's needs, then *how* they are defined, is crucial. Hitherto they have been defined *vertically*, in terms of the provision of specific services, welfare, housing, transport, etc, and coped with by separate departments with council committees to match. One of the objects of local government reform in the 1960s and 1970s has been to break this compartmentalization. A complete redefinition in *horizontal* terms, that is in terms defined not by the local services individually but with a sense of the interrelatedness of the conditions of life in particular areas of the city, would require, arguably, a more complete reworking of administration than is really likely and/or feasible. Nevertheless, since governmental activity is having more impact in horizontal terms, it is right to urge that the voice of the consumer/citizen at this level be articulated as clearly as possible. Secondly it is crucial *who* defines the needs. We have seen that the tradition in which city government has emerged has been one of, at its best, public-spirited administration by an élite, with the overwhelming majority of the citizens playing an almost totally inactive role. The main changes have been in the sheer bulk of responsibility undertaken, and in the character of the governing group. The social and business élite have to a large extent withdrawn, their places taken by men whose chief characteristic has been successful emergence in a party political structure. The political party has become the doorway to the town hall, and it has inherited the tradition. Latterly, however, we have seen the emergence into a dominating role of the official, the professional basing his claim to a place in the policy-making sun not on representativeness but on expertise. He and the politician now rule as a duumvirate, the balance of power between the two being variable from service to service and from town to town. While this highly problematic relationship is uneasily worked out, meanwhile the overwhelming majority of the citizens continue to have an almost totally inactive role. Attempts on the part of ordinary citizens, consumers of services, 'community activists', people affected by planning policies, to acquire a voice in the political process that affects them, involve them, among other things, in assaults upon a long and durable tradition.

A concluding note

Since 'the city' and 'society' in Britain today have become in one important sense almost synonymous, those who wish to reflect, in a general way, on cities and the conditions of urban living can easily be deflected up that meandering and inconclusive garden path formerly known as 'the condition of England' question. Cities *are*, in a sense, simply the chief and most obvious arenas where processes relating to the character of our society as a whole take effect. Yet they are not mere backgrounds. For, as units of government, they still have palpable and effectual identities and by what their governments do, and how they do it, cities can still contribute substantially to the making of their own futures.

The cumulative effect not only of millions of individual, private decisions and those of industry and commerce, but also of the policies taken by public authorities in exercising their responsibilities, determines the future of cities and the prospects of those who live in them. In considering the latter, however, it is not simply a question of arriving at the right priorities and implementing the right policies; we have to consider whether the political and administrative structures are capable of permitting this to happen. Here, whatever may be said at the national level, the potential power of that government which is conducted within the city boundaries is considerable, both in terms of the making of policies and the spending of large sums of money, and in terms of impact on the individual citizen at the receiving end. As local government's powers and duties expand and it departs further from its nineteenth-century role of providing some basic services and some modest ameliorative activity, twin contemporary problems come into the centre of the stage – the *effectiveness* of the machinery of urban government in meeting the city's needs, and its *responsiveness* to the citizens.

It was out of a perception of the malign human legacy of the nineteenth century that there grew the urge to use the machinery of government to engineer social and physical change. National governments everywhere are attempting, or being urged to attempt, the direction of the pace and character of urban development and redevelopment. The use of public power, however, may not produce intended consequences; since governmental capacity to control events is at best, limited, at worst, crude. Furthermore, whereas when dealing with highly disliked features of the legacy of the nineteenth century there was little problem of divergences of view between the decision-makers and the people, when 'planning' began to concern areas where no such consensus of value existed, the problem of what criteria and which people should provide the direction of policies and decisions became increasingly critical. Hence, Brian Berry notes 'perhaps the most important of the human consequences of urbanisation during the twentieth century may well be this attempt to change the nature of its perceived nineteenth-century consequences, to produce *by coercive means* more human urban environments.'[18] (My italics.)

The growth of power in the hands of city governments raises

in an acute form the issue of the meaning of democracy and citizenship in the age of giant cities. It is commonplace to note that we have come a long way from the Greek city-state so frequently held up in the past to be the model for democracy. How far, may be judged from the fact that the Athenian polis consisted of about 30,000 citizens – about enough voters to warrant 6 to 10 metropolitan district councillors. It is hardly surprising that for many people the gap between the ideals of democracy and the reality has become almost too wide to sustain credibility. In theory, we are supposed to fill that gap with the concept of representation, but for those oppressed by a well-grounded sense of powerlessness, the ability to assist in a minute way in electing a city councillor once a year is little consolation. In these circumstances, for people to stay away from the poll is at least as rational an action as to attend it.

We cannot evade the necessity of matching needs of a metropolitan scale with metropolitan sized resources and organization. Such democracy as we have achieved will be at risk if it cannot deliver the goods in terms of specific results in meeting needs. But it would be no less at risk, and more insidiously, if we were simply to call in the experts and bureaucrats and let them get on with it. Hence the need to explore new ways of breathing life into the concept of self-government, of the city as the public dimension of its people. Quite as much as urban government or the built environment, this old concept is in need of revivifying to match the conditions of a citified society. 'As if to mock us' writes Robert Dahl, 'the Latin roots of the word city remind us of what is most lacking in the giant city: citizenship.'[19]

Part Two **'Those Having Least Power':**
Urban Needs and Answers

> *... the residual location which is occupied by those having least power in the urban process.*
> – Oliver P. Williams; *on the 'ghetto'*[1]

> *In a letter written to me in 1883 Mr Ruskin told me that he believed that Manchester is simply an exponent of a given quantity of national guilt and folly ... this meant that Mr Ruskin believed that it is owing to the guilt and folly in every class of English people that there now exist in Manchester vast districts in which healthy life is impossible.*
> – Letter in the *Manchester Guardian*, 31 January 1901

In the early months of this century there was conducted in the columns of the *Manchester Guardian* a considerable debate on the causes of what were called 'our slums'. The view was forcefully expressed that they were caused by drink. A clergyman, writing from one of the areas in question, agreed, but added, as causes, such factors as unemployment and lack of education. One gentleman suggested the answer might be, not to build decent houses for the poor, but to build for the bourgeoisie on the country fringe of the city, so that their present houses could then pass down to the poorer classes. The whole debate makes sad reading today. Because of its patent inadequacy in face of the miseries that occasioned it; but even more because, 70 years on, it has still not been put to rest by our putting an end to bad housing and poverty. Oddly, it was Ruskin, writing, by proxy, from the grave, who made, if rather portentously, the most relevant and abiding point – that 'the poor' should be understood in the context of the rich. And the latter we can interpret as not just the upper 5 % but 'every class of English people' who, by virtue of income, political/trade union strength or whatever, have some power in the urban process – at least to gain for themselves decent housing and decent incomes with which to live in it. The failure of perception of those who wrote on 'our slums' and most of their successors for 70 years was to regard this as a 'problem' on its own, unrelated to the structure, social, economic, political, in which it was set. It is not, however, our purpose in the pages that follow to pursue the full implications of this; rather, to tackle the more modest task of identifying some of the main issues that have arisen in our post-war experience of tackling the legacy of urban deprivation, and to point to some of the things that need to be done.

Chapter 1 Housing

'Britain appears', writes Professor Donnison 'to be gradually incorporating a concern about bad housing conditions into its collective social conscience, alongside the concern for unemployment and medical care incorporated there a generation earlier.'[2]

Since the war no aspect of domestic programmes has absorbed more energy than housing. The country has been energetic in the provision of housing for its expanded and shifting population and in making up a very severe housing shortage, caused by the natural cessation of housebuilding and maintenance, during the war. Further, by the end of the war, of the existing housing stock of 11 million units, over half was more than 55 years old, so that there was a high replacement problem as well. In 1949 a PEP report estimated that two million dwellings needed demolition. In 1949 the government estimated a need to provide 750,000 houses for people with no separate dwelling and 500,000 for slum clearance and eliminating overcrowding. An energetic programme has gone a long way to meeting these needs and the country is now much better housed than it was in 1951.

No one would have thought, even fifteen years ago, that a quarter century of sustained effort and continual debate would have left us still acutely embarrassed over housing. By the late 1960s the government was able to claim that we had succeeded in creating a total housing stock in the country exceeding the number of households. It might now be said that Britain had not got *a* housing problem; but it *has* a series of specific and in places severe *local* housing problems, which bear down acutely on big city dwellers. The fit between what people want, or need, and what is available is often badly wrong. In inner London the problem is mainly caused by the dearth of private rented housing. In the inner areas of the provincial cities the problem has less to do with absolute shortage than with the poor physical and environmental quality of what is available. Even the claim to have achieved an excess of houses over households was rapidly falsified by the more recent slump in housebuilding. The reason we have failed to 'solve' the housing question is simply that it is a more complex matter than anyone in the immediate post-war years, seems to have imagined.

Housing is, as much as anything else, ultimately a product of people's financial capacity, the location and type of employment open to them, and the nature of the available transport network. As these have to a great extent influenced the city's housing pattern, these to a great extent hold the keys to its future. The sheer number of more immediately related variables to be taken into account in considering housing is one of the factors which renders effective policy-making very hazardous. There are the three broad sectors within which housing is provided (public, owner/occupier and private rented). There is the supply of land, the capacity of the building trade, regional land-use policy, building-society behaviour, subsidies, tax reliefs, rent policies and so on. Policy must also be based on forecasts of future population trends, and these have tended to alter quite substantially over the last decade or so.

Hence, as leading commentators such as Cullingworth and Donnison have pointed out, many different housing strategies are possible and there is great scope for conflict of values. The needs of the expanding and of the declining areas are one obvious source of conflict. Industry for new towns versus jobs for the inner city. The value of housing the most needy is not always compatible with that of replacing the worst houses, nor with the value of national minimum housing standards. Again, there are the presumed needs of future users of the housing who, the assumption runs, would require even higher than current minimum standards. The unborn generations, and the current planners who claim to speak for them, are an important factor in the slum clearance/improvement scene. Lastly, of course, the two parties have pursued different policies, the Labour party favouring extensive public enterprise through local authorities and the publicly subsidized rented house, while the Conservatives have supported the privately owned single family house in which the individual bears the responsibility, but in fact enjoys a concealed subsidy through the tax system. Housing has become, like education, a more contentious political issue over the years, reaching its peak, perhaps, in the 1972 Housing Finance Act, which embodied a radical departure from the concept of housing as a public service rather than a consumer good. There was here a clear, built-in preference for the marketplace which (argue its critics) if pursued to its conclusion, would have left public housing as a safety net for the poorest sections of society.[3] In 1974, Labour's Housing Rents and Subsidies Bill in turn reversed many of the 1972 provisions .

It may have been inevitable; it is certainly, surely regrettable, that housing should have become such a central battleground in the war of attrition between the parties and their respective constituents. Whichever party has held power, Britain's record of post-war housing effort as a percentage of gross national product has been relatively unimpressive, compared with Germany and Sweden. Low controlled rents and general under-maintenance have resulted in general slowness of improvement of the quality of the national housing inventory compared with what might have been, argues one critic.[4] And the country has spent less of its gross national product on housing in the early 1970s than it did in 1952.

Politicians have tended to use the statistics of housing construction as a yardstick of success. But it is the improvement of the quality of the total stock of housing in the country, or in any one city, which matters most. It took over 20 years for the point to be established that a blind concentration of effort on new house construction is not necessarily the best policy for achieving this end; and is, indeed one which victimizes the poor, in that the stock of housing cheap enough for their pockets has decreased markedly in recent decades largely as a direct result of the housing drive.

Since 1955 in the region of $1\frac{1}{2}$ million houses have been demolished in Great Britain. This has very substantial implications. In most cases it represents a direct swing in housing stock from private to public, thus placing more and more people in the hands, for better or for worse, of the public housing authority. About 30 % of the total housing stock in Britain (over 50 % in Scotland) is publicly owned and it is a steadily growing proportion. And, of course, 'clearance and redevelopment involve not only the replacement of old houses by new ones, they also involve the substitution of expensive houses for cheap houses. The rapid erosion of the low-price housing market has ramifications throughout the whole housing market.'[5] Only, Cullingworth notes, when we can say what the effect of clearance and redevelopment has been on the total housing market can we provide a firm socio-economic justification for slum clearance. In fact, so badly has the zeal for slum clearance been related to the general goal of meeting housing need that in the early 1970s several of the largest cities were demolishing houses far in excess of what were being newly erected.

Other factors besides decay and demolition have also contributed to the loss of cheap accommodation in inner cities. Students compete for it; in London especially, conversions to hotels, second homes for the wealthy, and the upper- and middle-class colonization, 'gentrification', of former working-class areas like Barnsbury all play a part.

The private landlord has played a critically important role in the housing market. The stereotype picture built up of him has obscured the picture. Even in London, 60 % of landlords let only one dwelling (though these only constitute 14 % of all rentings). And whether an honest citizen or a rapacious exploiter, he catered for a manifest need catered for in no other way, and his presence and activity *was* the consequence of housing policy. For decades there was only the weakest of machinery for effectively guarding against exploitation, yet at the same time, the private landlord was not provided with financial guarantees sufficient to induce him to invest in maintenance and improvement work. Hence we had created the situation whereby property degenerated to slum conditions under our very noses. Since the war most rents have been below the level at which essential maintenance could be done. Cullingworth showed that in Lancaster the council was spending on the maintenance of post-1918 housing a figure comparable to what many private landlords were obtaining in rent, regardless of the age of the housing.[6] With rent controls, soaring building costs etc. many landlords lacked any incentive to improve, while there were many local authorities so committed to the image of the racketeering landlord that they were not willing to assist any private landlord at all by putting public money into his pocket. The Milner-Holland Committee pointed out in 1965 that the private landlords' ability to improve the older stock was much hindered by their lack of assistance from the tax system – their tenants being the only group lacking any subsidy in one form or another for their housing.[7] This was also a theme of the Cullingworth report on Scotland's older houses which called for investigation of ways of financing private landlords so that they might undertake general improvement work.[8]

Nevertheless, the private landlord was able to provide a greater choice in housing than public authorities, for some people, especially for those needing large, or small, or cheap housing.

In England and Wales about 75 % of the privately rented accommodation dates from before 1919. Little new property has been built for private renting in the last 50 years, nor is more likely to be built. The rented sector accounted for 61 % of the housing stock in 1947, in England and Wales. By the 1970s it was 15 % and still falling. But it is this sector which has catered most effectively for the needs of the poorer very large and very small household. The older houses falling under the municipal bulldozer in recent years provided 49 % of the country's one and two roomed homes and 40 % of those with seven or more rooms (1964). Demolitions inevitably and swiftly whittle away at this stock. But the potential demand is greater than ever before. 15·4 % of all households consist of people living alone; two person households are about 30 % of the total. Usually the lowest cost of public sector housing has been substantially in excess of the cost of previous accommodation enjoyed by the tenants. Many authorities have operated differential rent schemes in which tenants paid a proportion of their income in rent (between one fifth and one ninth) – but often this disregarded family size, and there were some authorities not operating it at all.[9] For the poorest, council tenancy was simply out of the question.

The taking of this housing, at least temporarily, into local authority ownership is probably the surest, if not the only, way of ensuring the continuance and enhancement of the service this particular type of housing gives to the lower income groups. It is a weapon however that need not be used crudely. Where there is no threat of 'gentrification' or of exploitative landlordism it may not be necessary to use it at all. Where there *is*, as in inner London, authoritative opinion urges its wide use. Public acquisition of housing in stress areas will not create more housing; indeed it may reduce the quantity, by reducing density of occupation. But it will help to preserve the housing stock by providing for prompt repair and maintenance, and be the easiest means of providing security of tenure and a fair rent.

Three proposals in the Conservative White Paper *Better Homes; the Next Priorities* but dropped from both their and Labour's 1974 Housing Bills[10] would each have provided more help or protection to tenants. These would have required landlords selling rented property in housing action areas to offer the property first to a local council or housing association; allowed local authorities to nominate tenants for empty housing where the landlord had evidently not tried to find any; and required local authorities to rehouse tenants replaced by rehabilitation.

Public housing may be a social service; but like many of the social services it has not been a policy to seek out those in need, in contrast to those who have *applied* for public housing. Only in very recent years has the concept developed that the local authority ought to take responsibility for people other than those directly housed by them. The 1969 Report of the Central Housing Advisory Committee[11] on the purposes of council housing found that local authorities gave little thought to vulnerable groups in the private sector on the grounds that general housing policy catered for their needs. The Report endorsed Seebohm's recommendation that the local authority should take increased responsibility for housing the most vulnerable families, and in particular households in bad housing situations whose evident ability to cope was low. The difficulty is that as things stand, even if this type of household applies to the Housing Department, which is by no means always the case, it may be turned down as a 'poor risk'.

Cullingworth emphasizes that there is now in some areas a substantial eclipse of private enterprise and a situation of 'huge and increasing dependence'[12] on local authorities for the provision of decent housing. Glasgow has built over 100,000 homes since the war; conversely the private market built in the 1960s a mere 3 % of the city's homes. Among other effects this means that the segregation of the owner/occupiers from the council tenants becomes more marked; and that an ever-increasing proportion of the city's population are tenants of the corporation. This implies a huge concentration of power. The scope for bureaucratic overbearing is there, and there is plenty of evidence of authorities having exercised it – to bully applicants into not being too 'choosy' about the housing offered – to give the best houses to the 'deserving' i.e. the married, the unpoor. Parker concluded that many local authorities did not identify their poorest tenants largely because they used the crudest of measures of income. Little attention was paid to *per capita* income. 'The field of council rents is frankly chaotic. They are surrounded by untested assumptions, expediency, convention and lack of basic data . . .'[13] The Cullingworth committee on the practices of council house allocation noted that the more varied a council's own stock of property the more it seemed to see a necessity to sort out the people to suit the houses – a reversal of individual choice.[14]

The decline of the accommodation provided by the private landlord has meant, then, the threat of removal of the chief roof over the heads of many of the people about whom mainstream society, well organized in its public and owner/occupied sectors, does not want to know – coloured, poor, mobile, young and old. Local authorities, as the bodies mainly responsible for the destruction of the low cost private housing market, have a duty to see that there is low cost housing for those who had previously relied upon the private landlord.

It is glaringly obvious that this problem is not simply a housing problem but is a dimension of the poverty and inequality syndrome. Hitherto it has not been clear what part housing and the local authority *should* play in altering national income distribution. But the connection is there. Professor Donnison sums up the problem thus:

> The fundamental dilemma underlying most of our housing problems arises from a willing acceptance of great inequalities in the distribution of personal incomes, coupled with a rejection of similar inequalities in the distribution of housing ... a determination to provide decent housing for people now deprived of it cannot bear fruit unless they are enabled to pay for what they need.[15]

Clearly local authorities cannot, and do not see why they should, subsidize people through their housing revenue account. Yet, as Dr Spencer urges,

> To a large extent, the deprived housing situation of the poor results from the fact that it is the dwelling which is subsidised, whereas a strong case can be made for subsidising the people. Dwellings could then be more realistically allocated according to need, rather than according to the annual state of local authority housing revenue accounts and to a whole variety of points allocation systems which remain often inflexible and rarely provide a truly objective measure of housing need.[16]

Ultimately the entire housing system should be scaled for need rather than house type or housing sector. The pattern of tenure should reflect real needs and preferences and not arbitrary demarcations between the private and public spheres. Movement between these spheres should be easier, and there should be a greater role for non-profit making agencies. This might do much to shift the emphasis away from paternalism in the public sector and *laissez-faire* in the private, and towards a fuller orientation of the system towards consumer preferences. When people are poor they lack the means to act themselves, and are dependent upon planned public action, which is in turn channelled into certain directions by the structures of local government finance. In the absence of personal housing subsidy, some families cannot *afford* to move from inner areas out to overspill areas – the expense of new furnishings, and the subsequent expense of fares etc., would be too great. This is one factor whereby the social structure of some of the large new towns and overspill schemes is already predicated.

In an ideal world, people would be able to choose from a wide range of house types, designs, costs, locations and standards. Lack of choice applies of course not only to the public sector. The private sector is increasingly dominated by the larger builder, who produces as standardized a product as the local authority.

In fact, consumer preference has been given sadly low priority in the British housing situation. We have now had a variety of housing surveys both local and national, and have available a reasonable stock of information on housing conditions. We have also P. A. Stone's wide-ranging survey of housing needs for the next 40 years and the building industry's capability, under differing hypothetical conditions, of fulfilling its role.[17] With a few exceptions[18] though, we lack adequate information on peoples' own demands or expectations, their relative preferences for owner/occupation or renting, central city or suburban locations and so on. What does becoming an owner/occupier mean? What does it mean to put oneself on a council housing list – an act which in itself is easy and may signify everything or very little?

The existing stock of housing is the greatest source of choice of housing size, shape and location. Rehabilitating it offers great scope for providing variety at acceptable quality levels. And of preventing the appearance of more 'slums,' as well as avoiding the prolonged decline of neighbourhoods awaiting their turn in the clearance 'pipeline'. Besides, it is singularly crazy to aim to build 400,000 homes a year while we allow so much per year to dilapidate. 'A sensible housing policy', says Cullingworth, 'will therefore be heavily concerned with existing housing. To put the matter at its lowest, if existing houses are allowed to deteriorate into slums, they will need to be demolished and replaced at public expense.'[19]

In the early 1960s a scheme in Deeplish, Rochdale,[20] showed how an area that would earlier have gone the way of condemnation leading to demolition could be given new life by a plan of housing and environmental improvement. As in so many similar inner areas, most of the Deeplish landlords were elderly and not very well off. They lacked the energy to take advantage of grant aid for improving old properties. But most of the housing itself was structurally sound. What was necessary was to improve a few poorly maintained homes and to check the deterioration of the local environment. A range of improvements on a variety of levels of complexity was carried out. This proved to be only one early sign of a movement to replace wholesale redevelopment, where the structural conditions of the housing would permit, by a renewal of the environment, keeping the area socially 'in good heart'.

In 1967 the government did its own sample survey in England and Wales for the first time, and found that there were more houses in an unsatisfactory state than hitherto realized. Of the 13·9 million houses not actually unfit, some 3·7 million needed repairs costing £125 or more. These findings were published in the Ministry of Housing and Local Government's *Old Houses into New Homes,* in 1968. In this the idea was put forward of 'action areas' integrating housing and planning policies in a total urban renewal concept. The 1969 Housing Act enjoined authorities to be concerned with all unsatisfactory residential areas and not just slum clearance or council estates. The house improvement grant schemes initiated under this act, whatever their other effects, should, in the long run, help quite a lot to reverse the financial bias against the older house which has in the past accelerated tendencies to decay. If the houses over 50 years old (about which the building societies have been, on the whole, highly cautious) contain the vast bulk of Britain's 'unfit' houses, it is salutary to remember that 70 % of them are *not* 'unfit', yet.

As far as the private sector was concerned, however, the house improvement grants tended quite evidently, as with so many other well-intentioned acts of social policy, to help those with some existing capability rather than those in greatest need. Because it was based on a percentage, the grant was in effect, a subsidy to those already with some capital; it was used for second homes, and for fuelling speculative ventures by landlords to the detriment of the neediest would-be tenants. Hence by 1974 politicians of all parties were agreed on the need to put brakes on the use of these grants by those of means and to put the money into the areas of housing stress which they had not, hitherto, helped. A survey of London's housing needs found that although in 1972 improvements to older properties were running at nearly 30,000 a year, less than 35 % of these were in the 6 boroughs with the worst housing problems.[21]

House improvement was linked to the problem of the supply of cheap, private, rented accommodation by a recommendation from the Inquiry Report into the Greater London Development Plan (1973) that local authorities, with Ministry approval, should take on the improvement of dwellings for cheap renting where the private landlord was incapable, economically, of doing so. It rejected municipalization of the rented stock on the grounds that this would probably lead to a reduction in flexibility and variety of provision. But how, without public ownership, are we to ensure that, in some areas, this housing *stays* on the rented market, given all the existing pressures?

In its strategic housing plan (November 1974) the GLC proposed to rehabilitate property for tenants on a large scale. Birmingham's response was the designation of 60,000 properties for improvement in general improvement areas, with public health inspectors drawing up schedules of improvements and cajoling owners into grant-aided action. In Glasgow, the bed-recesses in living rooms of many tenements have made ideal spaces for conversion to bathrooms, and the corporation, in partnership with the Housing Corporation, has planned for improving up to 23,000 flats, both rented and owner/occupied.

The chief benefit of improvement is that it is an investment in the future well-being of a district and may help to prevent it having to be cleared, with all the attendant ills, in the future. Families, too, can live more cheaply, without being banished to the wastelands of the peripheral estates. Besides, multiple deprivation areas often stretch well outside the designated development areas. Environmental and social decay, failure to attract industry and retain young people, are problems often as acute in areas not facing *immediate* clearance as in those which are.

Much of the judgement between demolition and renovation must be technical and economic. It would make no sense to replace blind faith in demolition with blind faith in renovation. What is certain is that these judgements will have to be made for a very considerable period to come, unless much greater energy can be channelled into the big city housing programme.

In London, demolition of slum houses in 1972 was falling well below the minimum 7,000 per annum needed to keep abreast of the rate of obsolescence. Since so much of the cities, especially London, was built in the last quarter of the nineteenth century, and badly built at that, a substantial quantity of the housing stock is likely to fall into irretrievable decay over the next quarter of a century.

P. A. Stone, in his extensive analysis of Britain's housing needs and building capability for the next 25 years[22] argues that if the rate of construction were held at 375,000 p.a. (in the early 1970s the rate has fallen at times to less than a third of this, with the number of new houses declining steadily since 1968) and there was some slowing down on the drive for Parker-Morris standards, it would still, on 1964's figures, be the early 1980s before structurally unsound dwellings were replaced – and there has of course been deterioration since 1964. Hence, the importance of the contribution of improvement of existing houses.

We can, as Stone suggests, shift the direction of our housing effort. But he also indicates that there is little spare capacity within the housing sector, and capacity there can only be enhanced (aside from the continuing work of seeking greater productivity and the use of innovations in building technique) by deliberately intervening to direct building capacity to the housing effort and away from other activities. The growth of demand for non-residential building has been no less great than in the residential sector. But by no means all represents the same imperative need.

After the war Britain had an appallingly difficult legacy in big city housing to deal with. That it still has, so many years on, and despite all that has happened, is very much a mirror of wider failures in the political/economic management of the country's affairs. Housing has been the victim of ups and downs in policy, often of an ideological nature. Housing finance has been extremely complicated, with its difficult balance between the contributions of central government, rates, rents and tax reliefs; and it has of course been highly sensitive to fluctuations in the country's general financial fortunes. Planning delays and other bureaucratic obstacles have unnecessarily slowed the housing drive down. The construction industry has been used as an economic regulator. Much housebuilding is in the hands of small private firms who bob up and down on each wave of general economic fortune. In addition, local authorities, building societies, private landlords, housing associations and so on all contribute to the making of a confusion of agencies and pressures, the control and direction of which has so far proved beyond the capacity of government. Arguably, what is chiefly required of government is that it set the housing 'house' itself in order.

In October 1974, Lord Goodman, who had become chairman of the Housing Corporation, called for a Royal Commission to sort the housing mess out and untie some of the knots. The minister, in response, admitted that nobody had any clear idea, really, how many houses were needed. Promising a fundamental review of housing policy, he acknowledged the need to move 'beyond a policy of ad hocery and crisis management'.[23] An appropriate epitaph for a quarter of a century of housing policy.

Chapter 2 Deprivation

We must be very careful about the notion that deprivation is a 'city problem'. It can occur just as easily in rural areas, and it does. But it is characteristically in the inner areas of big cities that are to be found the densest clusters of what Weber called 'negatively privileged status groups'. This phrase is clumsy; but it does draw attention to a crucial and often conveniently ignored symbiosis – between deprivation and privilege. This is not to say that the poor are poor because the rich are rich. Modern society surely is not as crude as that. But there is a complex and subtle relationship, all the same.

Cullingworth defines poverty as 'relative lack of command over resources and access to opportunity'.[1] It is therefore not solely a question of money. Money that might secure adequate housing in one area might be quite inadequate in another. And the word 'relative' is crucial in the definition, for it focuses attention on the total social situation of the 'poor', the contrast between their resources and opportunities and those of others.

Deprivation has many faces. If we look at one face, others will show themselves. Housing is one example. It is only in recent years that bad housing has begun to take its place, beside the high unemployment and bad sanitation of earlier periods, as an intolerable national scandal. Hence it is only comparatively recently that we have begun to acquire decent estimates of the extent of housing deprivation in Britain. The Milner-Holland Committee's inquiry into London housing was the first comprehensive study of housing problems (albeit only in London) to be carried out by an independent committee since the Royal Commission on the Housing of the Working Classes in 1885. Since Milner-Holland the stock of our information has grown steadily and we can now etch out a profile of housing deprivation in Britain. The basic common denominator found in all the studies is low income. Further, it is well established that those in greatest 'objective' housing need and those who qualify for local authority assistance in one form or another are not necessarily the same sets of people. We know from the Plowden Report also that housing deprivation is correlated with comparative under-achievement in education – small, overcrowded homes lack play space, and may lack stimulation and security. Broken marriages are much more likely to occur. Health too may suffer, whether mental or physical or both. Areas of poor housing usually have low environmental conditions, with proximate industries, perhaps noisome or noxious, heavy through traffic, parked cars, etc. A child in South Kensington shares one tenth of an acre of play space with 8 other children; one in North Kensington shares the same area with 88 others. In short, as Spencer[2] puts it, 'Housing deprivation cannot be regarded in isolation, it is caused by and causes other forms of deprivation. It is logical, therefore, to propose that in the future housing policies should not be considered in isolation from other social policies, as has tended to happen in the past.'

The cumulative effects of deprivation are also pyschological. A sense of lack of competence, resulting in failure to take up such opportunities as are available; perhaps heavy indulgence in compensatory activities, for example teenage cults or gangs, and so on. In many cases these patterns of behaviour serve in the long run to stick the victim yet faster in the glue of his deprivation.

Some indications of the extent of relative deprivation in major cities may be gained by comparing the proportions of people lacking certain basic amenities in their housing in four inner wards of cities with the proportions for the cities as a whole and for the country as a whole, as found in the 1966 census. This reveals that the character of the problem differs from place to place. Especially the nature of the housing stock varies greatly from place to place and hence too the use that is made of it.[3]

	% large house-holds over 6 persons	% house-holds over 1½ per room density	% no use of hot water	% no use of fixed bath	% use of outside WC only	% house-holds in shared dwellings
GB	6·7	1·6	12·5	15·4	16·7	6·7
London	5·5	2·4	15·0	14·8	12·6	24·2
Islington	5·7	7·1	36·6	34·4	14·1	57·4
Barnsbury	7·6	10·3	44·6	51·9	18·1	
Birmingham	9·1	3·0	17·5	18·6	27·8	8·6
Soho	12·9	11·5	31·0	32·6	37·4	
Liverpool	11·4	2·6	20·2	25·6	31·6	8·4
Granby	12·8	10·1	41·0	42·8	40·5	
Glasgow	9·7	11·8	23·8	32·7	1·8	1·2
Woodside	8·0	21·5	54·9	76·7	4·2	

This, of course, is to compare the ward with the city's *average* – not with its most privileged wards and not with the most privileged areas of all which are often well beyond the city boundary.

In order to examine the specific situation in each ward it would be necessary to go more fully into the details of lack of amenity, such as the proportions having to share hot water and fixed bath facilities. In Woodside only 4·2 % had to use an outside WC, but 40·2 % of householders had to share an internal one, as against a national average of 4·4 %. In all four wards, the lack of basic household autonomy in respect of the major amenities of hot water, fixed bath and own WC was evident. In Islington, the basic framework of the problem was set by the sharing of dwellings by households, while in Woodside, it was the room density which was a more serious problem, as well as the chronic under-provision of washing facilities. To these areas too, of course, the coloured immigrants have come. With a national average of 1·6 % of population born in the so-called

'New Commonwealth', Soho, Birmingham had 21·3%. In Granby 6·6% of the residents were born in the 'New Commonwealth', in a city where the overall proportion was 0·7%. Like all newcomers, coloureds are low in the queue for public housing; some may have made perhaps ill-advised decisions in the private market; and they have, on account of colour and background, had special problems of their own.

The presentation of figures like these, which show the many-sidedness of urban deprivation, and its apparent concentration in certain severely disadvantaged inner wards, has fuelled the idea that there should be 'positive discrimination' based on territories of the city selected for priority treatment. Indeed this might appear such an obvious strategy that the problem has been only one of getting central and local government to make the effort. In fact, however, the issue is not as helpfully simple as it might, at first glance, seem.

These figures, by showing the different profiles of housing deprivation from one inner city ward to another, illustrate that many of the generalizations that can be made about deprivation, though valid in themselves, may be *too* general to give much of a lead in the adoption of specific policies. For example, the first and greatest indicator of general deprivation is social class, and specifically, in any particular area, the proportion of unskilled and semi-skilled workers. While these are more heavily concentrated in some areas than others, there is likely to be a spread of them over the whole city. Proceed further to the analysis of deprivation indicators and a similar pattern will emerge – some geographical concentration, some spread. And the distribution of the different deprivations may only show the crudest of overlaps – for instance between the poverty of the aged and underprivilege among schoolchildren. Certainly, in both cases we are likely to be chiefly talking of the 'inner area', but this is an enormous territory, in London involving whole boroughs. In 1966 over a million people were living in London wards with indubitably poor living and economic conditions: a population in London alone almost equivalent to that of Britain's second largest city. Again, in a recent study,[4] 16 indicators of deprivation were applied to the 21 wards in Southwark, and it emerged that only 2 wards failed to rank among the top 5 for at least one deprivation indicator. In other words, in Southwark the geography of deprivation is fairly widespread, involving, in fact, most of the borough. In Newham, by contrast, one of the 24 wards came among the first 5 on no less than 9 different indicators; here, perhaps, *is* a concentration so intense that a major discriminatory effort involving a fairly restricted territory might pay off. That is probably true of each of the 4 wards cited here; but only in very exceptional circumstances can we draw a sharp boundary distinguishing a heavily from a less-deprived area. One of the dilemmas of a priority area approach is likely to be therefore that to select a specific area for special discrimination is almost certainly to deprive the 'grey areas' on its borders of some share of the resources being made available, which they might have been entitled to on a pure 'needs' basis. We have seen this in operation in respect to, for example, the Educational Priority Areas. And this illustrates the more general point that direct intervention in a selected number of inner city areas, whatever its merits as a strategy in itself, cannot amount to, or substitute for, a comprehensive approach to the tackling of inequality and deprivation in society.

The concept of the disadvantaged or priority area is therefore vague. It tends to obscure rather than to clarify what should be done, in that it diverts attention away from the social structural factors, such as low income and the operation of the housing market, which cause people to *be* 'deprived'. And it does not, on examination, correspond very closely with the real world.

One last illustration of the point, in relation to the Educational Priority Area programme. J. H. Barnes[5] has observed that most disadvantaged children are *not* in disadvantaged areas and most of the children in disadvantaged areas are *not* disadvantaged. Moreover, policies of positive discrimination through schools, he says, will most benefit the *un*disadvantaged children in them.

If the priority area concept has a value it is not in itself but in the ideas with which it is associated – priority for primary education, the coordination of governmental effort, the involvement of local citizens in reinforced local institutions of their own, and so on. For if the idea of the priority area has been difficult to operationalize, it has at least called attention to acute needs and stimulated thought on how best to meet them.

Sadly, the action that it has impelled has, in relation to the dimensions of the need, been slow and puny, despite the idea's endorsement, in recent years, by most of the major government-initiated inquiries into urban social problems. The Milner-Holland Committee were well disposed to the idea of 'areas of special control' in areas of 'housing stress'. Plowden, on primary education, were the first to advocate a policy of 'positive discrimination', and, though chiefly concerned with education, saw schooling in poor areas as part of a cumulative deprivation syndrome. Seebohm too talked of areas of special need which should receive extra resources comprehensively planned.

Since these reports, several efforts made in this direction have been little more than gestures; others have been frankly experimental rather than involving major shifts in policy. In any case the universalist tradition on which so much social policy is founded could not easily be bent to a new principle. As a result of Plowden 'educational priority areas' were designated in 57 English and Welsh authorities. The Labour government set up an Urban Aid Programme for 'certain communities in areas of special need'. The Local Government Grants (Social Needs) Act, 1968, provided grants of up to £25 million for local authorities to finance special projects. This modest outlay was used mainly in furthering educational projects, such as nursery provision and language classes for immigrants. It developed further to embrace day centres for needy groups, housing aid centres and extra aid for general improvement areas. The government further embarked on its Community Development Project, the aim being, in 12 selected areas of high social need, to develop ways of coordinating existing services better and involving the people of the area in schemes evolving from their own felt needs. And Peter Walker in July 1972 announced 6 town studies designed to help local authorities develop a 'total approach', not wildly dissimilar in essence to that recommended to him by Shelter a few months earlier.

The EPAs, the Urban Programme, etc. might have held out the prospects of radical new departures in tackling urban deprivation. But they got minuscule funding in relation to the problems they were supposed to be addressing; and they have been subject both to political ideology and to the exigencies of national financial policy. They have been used as symbols of activity and concern rather than the substance; they have been used by governments as short term means of fending off criticism (e.g. over the effects of immigration). And the manner in which the community development projects were established clearly pointed to governmental lack of faith in local initiative. The project teams were controlled by central and local government personnel, plus members of the well-established and financially 'responsible' voluntary associations, and it was for the local services to operate 'solutions'. Holman comments that the potential of locally controlled movements to tackle social deprivation appears considerable, yet the Community Development Project has ruled them out from the start.[6] Local organizations, he comments, are rarely able to act directly on deprivation, but they are effective in helping members to obtain their welfare and housing rights, providing play facilities and pressurizing local authorities to provide facilities. The project has been aimed simply at making existing services better known and better coordinated, rather than to promote new strategies or initiatives. It is, it may be acknowledged, crucial that we make sure existing local authority and community resources are well used; but this is not enough. In so far as it is important that ways be devised of creating and mobilizing new community resources where few previously exist, this opportunity was not being explored in the official programme.

There is a great need for effective coordination, both on the ground in the affected urban areas, and at the level of national policy, of the various programmes such as the urban aid projects, community development projects, educational priority areas, etc.

'Area management' is a method of coordinating the local services and other projects in relation to the needs of a particular district. It is not a means of pumping extra resources into an area but does aim at getting for the area a better share of existing resources and a more sensitive use of them. Although essentially a management device of the council, the model scheme for an area of Liverpool (where one of the first DOE sponsored experiments was initiated) envisaged an area management committee of councillors and possibly others to cater for local opinion.[7]

In its proposal to the government in March 1972 Shelter urged a vigorous approach on priority area lines – the General Development Area. This called for a government financed programme for specific, recognizable geographical entities in the inner cities. There would be special, coordinated programmes of housing, social service, educational and environmental improvement. Financial and analytical resources would be provided for identifying problems, a job which would require task forces of specialists from sources including the government departments, universities, local authorities and private firms. In each General Development Area there would be a local service centre to give information on all services and programmes in the area; a professional community organizer; a local manager of assistant town clerk status, reporting directly to the town clerk or chief executive, his function being to coordinate the planning and delivery of services and to develop programmes; and finally there should be in each area a local advisory group of local representatives. As they saw it, the programme differed from traditional practice in being *selective* as to areas, *comprehensive* in approach and *catalytic* of self-help and institutional initiatives.[8]

It was notable that this proposal was very closely linked to emphasis on changes in the internal management of local authorities to ensure more stress on programmes than on services or professions, and better coordination of activities at the resource allocation stage. Current changes in the management styles of local government are geared to this end; nevertheless there are critics who would argue that local authorities, restyled or no, have not proved other than highly suspicious of all efforts at regeneration of deprived areas that have not taken place strictly under their own umbrella. This was one of Dearlove's main findings in Kensington,[9] while one of the Shelter Neighbourhood Action Project's final reports comments that with respect to its own activities in the Granby area of Liverpool, high initial resident enthusiasm began to wane as the city council proved 'unable to discuss any commitment to total proposals for deprived areas in terms meaningful to residents'.[10] Some local authorities simply lack the desire to apply for help for their poor areas; others may not consider they can afford the input they are required to make, or may be unable to mount the exercise needed to make a detailed application based on a plan. Even so, many bids to improve areas of negative privilege have had to be turned down, thus pointing the inadequacy of the funding made available by the government.

The difficulty of acting to combat urban deprivation lies in the very interrelatedness of social life itself. There is only limited value in providing play-schooling if a child returns to a deprived housing situation and will attend a poorly favoured primary school later. The complexity of need demands a good deal more for its combating than ignorant goodwill and energy (though it will certainly need the latter). If we are to pursue interventionist policies to combat deprivation these must be based on a fuller understanding of it than we have at present. This entails considerable further effort to develop reliable indicators of social characteristics, their correlates, and geographical distribution, as well as the development of the theoretical frameworks without which these would be simply clusters of statistics. An important part of this work, too, must be the evaluation of the performance of any programme of positive discrimination that is adopted. We have seen often enough in the past how good intentions alone have tended to be regarded as adequate justification for particular policies. Various evaluative exercises are in process, but this is a very new activity for which even the tools have to be fashioned.

In conclusion

It is obvious that while there may be those who suffer merely a housing problem, a colour problem, a poverty problem, the major issue is the existence, throughout the city but chiefly in the inner districts, of a deprivation syndrome in which many people suffer an accumulation of disadvantages. To these we must add political powerlessness. It is obvious too that to think of these as 'problems' 'caused' by the cities is to obfuscate the issue. The city is not a monster with a will of its own distributing benefits to some, disadvantages to others. As the causes lie in the character of society as a whole it is only within that context that a true 'solution' is possible. At the same time, our society *has* placed upon the cities as governmental institutions a considerable responsibility as vehicles for the conduct of social policy. We must make sure these are instruments for amelioration and not for making things worse.

What, then, shall we do? The deprivation syndrome is such that action based on any one approach and aimed at one problem alone – housing, education, etc. – is likely merely to succeed in changing the dimensions of the difficulty. We have had enough of compartmentalized policy-making, and it does not meet these needs. At the same time, calls for a 'total' approach tend to be too unspecific to be helpful. There is a call for a national urban policy, but it is not generally very clear what this should consist of. More to the point would be an effective, and coordinated, package of policies for tackling low income, poor employment opportunities and the inequities in the provision of housing across the country as a whole. And this has other, specific, implications for national policy. For instance, it is not possible to have an effective policy for dealing with housing and poverty in inner areas without having an effective policy for land. The Labour Party in the 1960s, with its Land Commission, had, as it were, its heart in the right place, but its head was a long way behind, since the role the Commission was to play had clearly not been thought through adequately. Nor is such a policy possible without some over-riding of existing local government jurisdictions. The inner boroughs of London must have access to land in the outer boroughs, and this is one reason for the call (by the Culling-worth, Greve and Layfield reports) for a Metropolitan Housing Authority. Housing need is no respecter of local authority boundaries.

Research on poverty suggests that in many cases it has made precious little difference to the poor which party has been in power. The value of the wages of the poorest 10 % of male manual workers, as a percentage of average male manual workers' earnings was 71·6 % in 1964. By 1970 it was 67·3 %, by 1974 61·3 %. The gulf has widened steadily,[11] under govern-ments of both main parties. And low income is really the key to much else. Educational research, for example, tends strongly to point to parental occupation as the most powerful outside factor affecting children's educational performance.

So is it better to try to improve the housing, or to improve the incomes and job opportunities of those who inhabit it, so that they in turn will have the chance of improving the houses themselves or of exercising some choice in the housing market? Again, many of the low paid cannot afford to live far from their work, yet at the same time land-values near to their work may be high and hence so may be the cost of their housing. Here, an attack on the location of jobs, the provision of really cheap and efficient transport (thus widening people's choice of housing location) and a tackling of urban land-values may be more relevant than a direct attack on 'housing' itself.[12]

The priority area, the general development area, the 'total' approach may have been turned to in response to a feeling that urban deprivation has proved too complex and intractable for governments operating along more conventional lines to cope with. Complex it is, but arguably the difficulty has been, not that government policy cannot reach the 'submerged tenth' but that the right policies to do so have not been adopted (for whatever reason).

The community development and priority area approaches are worth persisting with for their own sakes, vague as they might be, if only to ensure for national and local policy the maximum efficacy at the point of impact. Local authorities must be so organized and managed as to have maximum effectiveness, and in particular they must be capable of overcoming their own inherited and to some extent inbuilt tendencies towards fragmentation of policy applying effort. This is what the new corporate management is designed, in theory, to do.[13] Finally, there must be a new role for the neighbourhood and its people themselves. Because what has been said implies an even bigger governmental impact on their lives than before, there must be countervailing local defences against bureaucratic domination. And, because the local community's own latent capabilities are too valuable a resource to squander.

We need, therefore, action at several levels. We need effective policies at the national level on low income, land-values, employment opportunities, where there are general needs in society but which are particularly severe, and cumulative in the inner urban areas. In these areas we need to 'top up' with further developments of the territorial approach. We need effective and imaginative management and policy-making at the local governmental level. And we need the energies and local knowledge of the people themselves. Nothing less is likely to be sufficient.

A note on 'twilight zones'

Various terms have been coined in the attempt to describe these areas, and most of them are only partially useful. 'Twilight zone' is one, 'zone of transition' another. These are imprecise, and even misleading. 'Ghetto' is worse, since this word is now popularly used to describe anything from an area lived in *by choice* by an ethnic group, or even a class group (as in 'middle-class ghetto'), to an area lived in by people too powerless to have *any* alternative choice at all. Richard Sennett, in his *The Uses of Disorder*[14] calls attention usefully to the complex social relationship between the people of the city as a whole and those of the so-called 'twilight zone' as being characterized by 'purification'. Those who are 'impure' are thus not only those who *cannot* secure acceptance in a 'purified' community but also those who would *choose not* to.

A striking feature of the development of the large city is its segregation into districts each distinctive in social character from its neighbours. Segregation has always existed, of course, and many types could be cited both in pre-industrial cities and in rural life. The tendency towards differentiation has merely intensified in the large industrial city, with both individual choice and the public authority housing drive playing a part. As a result a majority of citizens live now in what Sennett calls 'purified communities', that is, neighbourhoods purged of the disturbing presence of outsiders who might represent something different from, or even in conflict with, whatever confirms local solidarity. And as Sennett argues, this is not merely a physical segregation, it is psychological, leading to patterns of avoidance and group antagonism, the desire to keep the purification going by resisting the territorial claims of outside groups. Every city can provide examples of housing estates as big as medium-sized towns comprised almost exclusively of skilled manual workers, or suburbs exclusively white collar, and with a few favoured by and only affordable by 'executives' and higher ranking professionals.

It is natural for people to want to live like with like. No one should deprive them of the choice. However, this differentiation of the city into purified communities has serious implications. We have noted earlier the extremely grave implications for the British core city of present tendencies especially as they affect social needs and public resources. The 'twilight zone' is, in a sense, the residual zone, the dumping ground of the city, where live a high proportion of those who have not the qualifications for acceptance in any purified community (such as the coloured, the poor, the mobile young), who are, in effect, the 'impure', and who precisely because of that have not the political muscle that they need in order to achieve anything in the play of city politics.

The process of purification and its corollary, the dislike of the 'impure' has its impact on the mentality of city bureaucracies and political élites. These attitudes have resulted in city corporations *either* trying to keep the impurity penned in a specific area and preventing it from 'spreading' *or* attempting to sweep it all away in one fell plan.

Redevelopment and renewal policies ought to be sensitive not only to the needs of the older inner areas but also to their *uses*. They may contain people trapped there by poverty and lack of power; but they also contain people who chose to live there for the sake of cheapness of housing, ease of access to the centre and to work, or nearness to family and friends. If such areas contain many people with 'problems' we should remember that ten times more people are more likely to be leading a perfectly 'normal' life than not. It is a matter for respect that the majority of people, given adverse conditions, manage to remain resilient.

Many find in these areas a privacy and anonymity which a more purified community might deny them. They provide room for private experimentation. The back-street workshop, the junk-shop owner, the second-hand furniture dealer, the scrap-metal man; this is their territory. Here a thousand odd trades, crafts and services can be carried on to nobody's harm and the general enhancement of the city's life. We must continue to have areas of cities where everyone of modest means needing premises to carry on creative activities from entertainment to poetry to invention, may find them. We must, if we are civilized, recognize the contribution such an area makes to the texture of urban living. Let us then be sure we are not loosing the municipal bulldozer against people, places and activities whose only sin may be that they are shabby.

The existence of grime, the proximity of bad environmental

elements such as smell-emitting industries do *not* amount to evidence of decay or grounds for wholesale demolition. They may simply mean that efforts ought to be directed towards removing environmental *causes* rather than the houses and people who happen to suffer the effects. Medhurst and Lewis put it thus:

> In the middle of a bad environment there may easily be a building, or a whole street of buildings, in good condition . . . the person who looks superficially at an area and describes it as a slum . . . may quite overlook the condition of the buildings, and if the main fault in these is external grime he may go away advocating a policy for slum clearance that would entail the demolition of a high percentage of sound buildings.[15]

Policies for the physical fabric of inner areas require, above all, understanding of their physical and social dimensions and the linkages between them. The causes and interrelationships are extremely complex. The physical fabric of our cities has a natural tendency towards decay; that is the other side of the coin of change. Presumably we want to remove the irrecoverably decayed, then to prevent decay from spreading where it is not wanted; but also (and this is where sensitivity to the variety of citizens' needs comes in) to halt it at *an acceptable level of decadence* to provide us with places where the *uses* of decadence can be valued.

Part Three **City Government in Transition**

Chapter 1 Problems of Reform

> *... the only machinery by which we can effectively secure our needs.*
> – Joseph Chamberlain, 1875[1]
>
> *It was put to us in evidence that our objective must be to make democracy as efficient as possible, not to make efficiency as democratic as possible, and there is a good deal of truth in this.*
> – Bains Report, 1972[2]

As recently as 1967 Professor William Robson was able to write that 'one of the oddest facts of our time is that practically none of the political leaders of the twentieth century has shown any interest in strengthening local government or even in helping it to survive'.[3] In the few years since then, we have seen more changes in the structure of local government than in the previous eighty. It hardly needs rehearsing here the details of how the basic system created in 1888, complained of by Professor Robson as 'too durable, like Victorian houses or furniture' was replaced by a new one taking over in England and Wales in April 1974; which, among other things, took account, however oddly, of the obsolescence of the former town/country distinction, and gave a special status to the largest 'metropolitan' areas in England and Wales other than London. This has been the most outward and visible sign of change; but it has not been the only one. The considerations which are aired in the discussion ensuing refer to a set of changes quieter but at least as significant – those involving the internal structures of local government. Here, much reshaping has been taking place according to new concepts of managerial efficiency; and these in turn have raised in a new form an old question – what part is there for the elected representative to play, and what sort of man or woman is a 'fit and proper person' to play it? At the back of all of this, too, lies the most fundamental question of all – what is local government for?

During the reform period, there has been evidence of substantial muddle as to the answers to these questions. Indeed, in the first place, it is not easy to understand why after most of a century there *was* suddenly such a flurry of concern and activity in the late 1960s. One possible answer lies in the general mood that followed the failures of Mr Macmillan's later years. As a substitute for Europe, and for a world role, a quest for national efficiency did not have much appeal, but it was, perhaps, one of the few options open. Hence élite circles (though not the rest of the country) became for a time seized with an enthusiasm for modernization and change, almost for its own sake. Then, from 1964, Labour were in power, and that party has always regarded its experience in local government as one of its stronger suits. At the same time, the United States was undergoing many well-publicized anxieties about its 'urban crisis'. It is notable that little such sense of crisis invaded the calm of the British debate. Attempts, such as those of Shelter, to link urban *government* with the acutest urban social *problems* did not break through the apathy with which most otherwise socially alert people viewed local government. This was a great pity, for it meant that discussion of the future of urban government was confined to fairly specialist circles. In the end, it was by no means as clear as it should have been what the objectives of local governmental reform ought to be. There was a desire for 'efficiency' and better planning; some people desired a local government system more robustly independent of the central government; the rather vague hope was often expressed that somehow these values, if enhanced, would lead to greater citizen involvement. But it could be argued in retrospect that this muddle of good intentions was never really sorted out. Arguments for 'economies of scale' were unhesitatingly accepted, those on 'diseconomies of scale' were ignored. The question 'efficiency for what?' was not asked often enough. As Jeffrey Stanyer has shown in a scathing critique, the Redcliffe-Maud Commission not only cast the values behind the intended local government reform in ambiguous terms but also, far from drawing the obvious conclusions from available research evidence, including its own, continued to repeat, and base its findings on, discredited clichés.[4] If this was so of the body specifically charged with the task of analysis and recommendation regarding the system as a whole, the same was always likely to be true of the end product, of reform legislation itself, when party political considerations were added in as well.

Justifying its existence

Only now, and largely too late to affect the reshaped system, are we getting theoretical discussion concerning the proper role and functions of local government in a modern democracy.[5] Hitherto, there had been little to speak of since Mill's essay on Representative Government was published in 1861. We have had, at best, what W. J. M. Mackenzie calls 'an ethical commitment to an extremely vague notion of local self-government'.[6]

In a comparatively small country like Britain, with a long tradition of strong central government and (by world standards) a fairly homogeneous population, it would not be unreasonable, *prima facie*, to argue that all decisions and administration should be centralized at Westminster. Indeed, there is much to be said for it. The greater the devolution of power away from the centre the greater the scope for the growth of territorial inequalities. As it is, along with talk of greater regional devolution, there is increasing pressure on central government to intervene on behalf of hard pressed areas like London and the stress areas of the provincial cities. Financially, the proportion of local revenue coming from central grants has been increasing over many years. Yet the commitment to local government remains, so much so that vast efforts are put into reshaping it.

Local government is more than a mere field agent of central government. This would be one possible role for it to play; but clearly the relationship between central and local government is more complex than that. It *is* an agent of central government, carrying out tasks laid down by Parliament, but it is, at the least, one charged with the task of tempering its activities to local opinion as expressed through the representative system; and this is an important modification. Besides, the directives of central government are often either somewhat general and imprecise in character or are simply advisory. There is plenty of room in which coherence and purposiveness have to be forged. Nor, at the local level, is the task that of a straight-forward administrative organization. There is no market mechanism to provide guidelines, if not imperatives. Admini-strators have to work with politicians, and vice versa. The presence of an electorate represents, for both, perpetual uncer-tainty. In short, it is easier to detail what local government is *not* than what it *is*. It is not, therefore, surprising that 'there is much less clarity and aim of purpose within the local authority than many other kinds of organisation'.[7]

If local government is not a mere agent of central govern-ment, what, then, is it? W. J. Money[8] suggests two other possible answers. One, that local government is simply *sui generis* – it is what it does. That is to say, that there is no very clear or logical distinction possible between the activities of central and local government, and that the latter simply *is*, and would be best left to adapt and muddle through changing times, in the confidence that this, in the past, has worked well enough. Two, that local government is an expression of a democratic 'natural right'. Local government is, for local people, a kind of 'do-it-yourself' government and is hence a realization of one of the fundamental concepts of democracy, self-government. Money's clear preference is for the latter view, and he warns that the continuance of the 'pragmatic' model of local government is likely to lead to greater losses of power to the centre, so that in practice there may be little difference between the 'pragmatic' model and a mere agency carrying out central government administration 'with a human face'.

In another review of the theories and values of local govern-ment which have been, or might be, advanced, L. J. Sharpe[9] suggests that local government has been justified firstly as an aid to liberty; secondly as a means of public participation in government; and thirdly as a means of providing efficient services to the local community. Of these, evidence suggests the first is, at best, merely an extra or bonus, and while the second *may* be valid, in practice its value often tends to lie in the area of promise rather than achievement. These arguments would be stronger in a large country with many people living far from the capital, and in one with substantial and distinct minorities. Historically and today, British local government is chiefly there to provide services, and to provide them in a way which, being local, could not be done by central government. Success or failure must be measured by the quality and efficiency of service provision.

Arguably district commissioners could do this just as well. In order to 'know' local conditions and needs it may not be necessary to have the mystical communion with a district sometimes claimed by councillors. (Indeed the pride and self-justification of being locally born and bred which many actors on the local scene, from councillors to journalists, evince, is self-revealing. Much of the running in local politics is made by people who have never had their childhood prejudices and attachments to ways of doing things shaken up by the experience of living elsewhere.) Nevertheless district commissioners would *not* do, for their use would offend against the argument for democracy as self-government, at local level. The jobs of coordinating services, adjusting them to the particular needs of each community, and accommodating what Sharpe calls the 'subjective views within the community as to what the objective facts imply in terms of need,'[10] are uniquely ones which central government has neither the time nor capacity to cope with, either on its own or through a system of agents. And it is when the argument shifts from local needs to local *perceptions* of need that the democratically elected representative comes into the centre of the picture. Efficiency in service provision cannot be an end in itself. As Money argues, local government *can* be democratic *and* efficient – but only if we insist that unless policy making and service provision *are* democratically controlled by local representatives they are *not* being conducted efficiently according to the purposes implied.

in the concept 'local government'. Hence the question of whether a policy is carried out democratically is, in this argument, at least, as important as its inherent qualities as a policy.

But how are we to see to it that policy making *is* subject to effective local democratic control? This raises two questions, concerning the sort of representative best suited to carry out this task, and the sort of structure which best combines effective administration with effective democracy.

Councillors – what for?

What, then, are elected representatives for? In the run-up to reform the idea was much canvassed that local government operates well below capacity in its ability to attract men and women of calibre into local government service – a situation which would be changed if the nature of the system were changed. The Maud Report (1967) laid stress on the dearth of 'quality' people in almost all of the authorities it examined. Dame Evelyn Sharp, Permanent Secretary to the Ministry of Housing and Local Government said in 1962 that 'part of the trouble in getting enough good people to serve arises . . . from the fact that the areas and status of local authorities are often today too cramped or too small to enable a satisfactory job to be done'.[11] The Maud Report (1967) endorsed this view when it summed up its reform proposals with the hope that 'the freedoms we advocate for local authorities, together with increased financial autonomy and more powerful local authority units would, we believe, do much to attract people of calibre to the service of local authorities'.[12] The Maud Report (1967) emphasized internal reorganization and a reduction in the number of councillors, thus leaving fewer councillors with a bigger, better defined task to do. The Redcliffe-Maud proposals (1969) aimed at the same effect with regard to areas and functions. It was hoped there would be 'fresh encouragement for citizens to take an active and effective part in their own local government, and new vitality can thus be breathed into our local life'.[13]

The question of the fitness or quality of city councillors has been, as we have seen elsewhere, a hardy annual for over a century. As E. P. Hennock shows[14] for example, in the 1850s there was repeated criticism that a change for worse had taken place since 1835. What this meant in substance was that the 'more respectable inhabitants' had been replaced by merchants and tradesmen. The linking of 'quality' in a councillor with high social standing in the community has been remarkably persistent. Lord Simon in 1921 as Mayor of Manchester repeated the hope that an improvement in the city's political life would follow an extension of the city's boundaries to include some affluent Cheshire suburbs.[15] Of course, all this begs the question, 'fitness for what?' Since that in turn depends on what the main task of the council is conceived to be, it might not be unreasonable to expect the answer to differ from one time to another. As we have seen[16], Hennock suggests, for example, that in the nineteenth century, a council full of 'men of substance' was suited to the task of managing corporate property, but that when the spending of rates became a central concern, it was to be expected that they should cede place to a 'shopocracy' highly sensitive to economy.

Be that as it may, developments in this century have greatly changed the function of the council and its administrative profile. The rise of the professional administrator has replaced the large entrepreneur as the locus of managerial expertise in Town Hall; while the council has increasingly been concerned with the provision of services. Fitness to serve as a councillor is, therefore, not fitness to duplicate the managerial and professional skills which the council now acquires through its paid officials, but fitness to direct and scrutinize their activity.

There will thus have to be those who can express and impose political will and who can, if necessary, wheel and deal. And there will have to be those who can articulate the needs of the consumers of local authority services. For these activities there are no doubt certain criteria of fitness; but they are not the preserve of any particular social class or status group.

The assumption that there was a pool of talented potential

councillors ready to emerge once the system became attractive to them, is a strange and interesting one. There are several grounds for sceptism as to whether this was a reasonable expectation in the first place. There is now considerable evidence as to what councillors actually do, and it leads us to question whether councillors really are frustrated decision-makers as Maud rather suggested they were. Many of those who, before reorganization at least, were attracted to take up council work were so because of an urge to secure specific improvements in local services. The communications they received from the public were exclusively, according to one survey in Manchester[17], about grievances, not policy. Over half the councillors surveyed, said their biggest source of satisfaction was in giving personal assistance over people's housing problems, getting improvements to old people's homes or bath tubs for cripples, and similar direct and personal tasks in the councillor's own locality. In short 'reforms isolating councillors from the more human details of government in favour of analytic, deliberative tasks would probably make the councillor's job much less attractive to many potential and valuable councillors'.[18] Only 17 % of Manchester councillors had any specific policy goal at all.

When it comes to a matter of policy-making, the councillor is faced with a task for which he may not be very well equipped. In most cases he 'has taken off an afternoon from his private occupation and faces in the committee meeting an officer who has worked for years in a particular field and who is backed by the resources of an entire department'.[19] No wonder then that many elected representatives have tended to latch on, with relief, to the pursuit of graspable, if petty, details. One councillor said that 'I've sat in meetings where we argued an hour about £100 for traffic wardens' shirts and passed a £5,000 scheme without a murmur'.[20] One might conclude, with the author of this survey, that they *choose* to get bogged down in detail because of the heavy demands of comprehending more central issues. Professor Walsh indeed points to the paradox that, the world over, interest groups, and elected representatives tend to exert more influence on issues traditionally considered administrative, such as appointments, contracts and legal proceedings, than they do on basic policies.[21]

Not only was there evidence to suggest that councillors were often happier in the personal service side of their activity than in their relationship to power and decision-making, but many have held a fairly modest view of what they are there for. The majority do not mention power or influence as a personal objective, and few say that is what they would miss if no longer on the council. Under the outgoing system a nearness to where decisions were made, a sense of being 'in on' things, was of paramount importance to many. Even on the council 'the spectators of the power game are much more numerous than those who act in it, even if hard work is the price one has to pay to attend the performance'.[22] For that matter, some councillors, according to one survey, may see the town hall as simply the 'best club in town'.[23]

There appears to be some marked difference, between members of the two major parties, as to the extent of leeway that should be given by councillors to officials. The Conservatives, being perhaps the less programmatic party, appear much more disposed to let officials have their heads, whereas Labour councillors are more likely, on the whole, to attempt to impose their wills. For instance, Hampton found in Sheffield[24] that 88% of Conservative councillors agreed that councillors should leave the day to day running of affairs in the hands of officers and should confine their own activities to broad policy matters. Labour councillors were much more disposed to be suspicious of this proposition, for only 62% agreed with it and 27% 'very strongly' disagreed. Among Labour committee chairmen agreement dropped to 55% and 'very strong' disagreement rose to 35%. There was a Labour feeling that councillors could not control policy without detailed knowledge. Boaden's study of policy-making in English county boroughs confirms this tendency.[25]

These rival interpretations of the functions of councillors were to some extent reflected in the recommendations of the

Maud and later the Bains Reports. The respective party dispositions reflect a difficulty for which there is no neat resolving formula. On the one hand, councillors need enough of a sense of detail to be able to cope with the activities of fact-armed officials. On the other, over-immersion in detail has even more obviously undesirable effects – expense of time, the losing sight of the wood for the trees, etc. Hitherto, this has probably been the greater danger. As one Sheffield alderman remarked, 'one of the weaknesses of elected representatives is their tendency to tell the park-keeper how to cut grass'.[26]

Council work is costly to those who participate in it. Even councillors themselves report serious deterrent factors. 80 % of Manchester councillors felt that the greatest drawback was the amount of time the work consumed. They spent a range of 36 to 100 hours a month.[27] The Redcliffe-Maud Report gave an average in county boroughs of 76·6 hours per month.[28] The monthly 3 to 4 hour city council meeting was perhaps the only part of this that 'showed', but a large proportion of time was consumed by committee meetings and party work. There was a great variation in the amount of time taken up by consultations and 'surgery' activities for constituents, depending on the nature of the ward (almost all requests for help deal with housing problems), and on the temperament and attitude of the councillor himself. Even so, half the Manchester councillors felt unable to spend as much time as they needed to on council work. 'Cases' could crop up anywhere – in the pub or at a dance, so that the well-known councillor's only really 'free' time was when he was out of his borough. More than a third – and even more of those who left the council voluntarily, felt that it had interfered with their business and family life. In fact more people left the council for this reason than for old age and ill health. Over half the councillors felt, and could substantiate, that it had harmed their careers – particularly those employed by private enterprise. Many could cite loss of income in actual figures. Even if we allow something for self-dramatization these are substantial hazards. Often it has been those who might have most to contribute who have had to give up while the drones continue. Labour councillors from safe wards often suffer most in economic hardship. Having safe seats they tend to become chairmen and have to assume extra responsibilities, in addition to being subject to the heaviest demands from constituents. At times committee chairmen may have to spend several days a week just to keep prepared and up to date on their papers. In return councillors often feel they gain little in respect for their work. Until 1974, however, the aldermanic system has relieved some of the pressures from key members, by relieving them of the constituency dimension. This was abolished with the reform of the system.

An unfavourable image plus the real penalties of time consumed, and work and career prospects dimmed, is an important deterrent factor.

In the plea for a better calibre of councillor there frequently may be detected an assumption that businessmen and professionals would make a better job of it than housewives, small shopkeepers and trade union officials. Be that as it may, R. V. Clements[29] reports on a survey of 78 of the most prominent of the business leaders of Bristol that 77 % of them gave the excessive time that would be required as their major reason for not seeking to join the local council. Clements comments that this is somewhat spurious, as many 'notables' are very willing to sacrifice time for voluntary charitable activities such as welfare bodies, the independent schools and the cathedral building fund. Almost as powerful an objection and one voiced by 68 % of the sample was a dislike of party politics in local government. It 'ran through many interviews as a sort of refrain'.[30] Indeed, only 19 % did *not* at some stage in the interviews make a derogatory remark about party politics in local government. This antipathy may be a particular characteristic of businessmen rather than people in general, but it is more likely that it is simply one version of a widely felt attitude. Well over half of the Bristol businessmen could not imagine *any* change of *any sort* in the local government system which might lead them to change their attitude to being council candidates.

Clements puts forward the theory that business leaders are used to a certain autocratic way of life in their businesses; and that this brings them to view the give and take of politics with distaste. Hence it is unlikely that changes in the way of conducting council business would alter their disposition to remain aloof.

All this matters only to those who feel that top businessmen and professionals (a) have unique qualities and (b) should be induced to come forward to lend these to the cities. This is not a sustainable view. As Clements points out, local government, poor as its record on participation might be, does provide one of the few means of allowing ordinary people to attain a measure of political power. They should not have to cede yet more room to groups which already have a substantial share of power and privilege. Moreover, the council does not lack managerial and professional advice, since it is on tap in the persons of the officials. Finally the argument for 'quality' people implies a particular view of the local elected representative which is a managerial rather than a political one. To put it forward is to misunderstand the demands of democratic government in the same way as those do who call for throwing out the politicians at Westminster and installing a government of businessmen.

However, while the position of business leaders may have elements distinctive to themselves, it is more than probable that many, if not a majority, of people, share their other objections to council participation – such as those on grounds of time demanded, or the claims of other, more congenial, areas of activity. The present spread of people active in local government and politics is a minority produced by a filtration process which predisposes out the vast majority of the population. The hope, then, that there is a large and tappable pool of 'high calibre' potential local government representatives is probably unfounded.

Most of the arguments for reform that centred on this point rested on the belief that what was needed to provide a new dynamic to local government was new management, both in the sense of organization and of men. Management is an important part of government; but government is not management. If more attention had been paid to the purposes management in local government was to serve, a better perspective might have informed the proposals.

There was no denying the need to serve the ends of local government by the best structures possible. Time wasting procedures, time-consumption on trivia, inefficient methods of decision-taking are detrimental both to representative democracy and to the substantive ends of service provision. But to turn councillors into a minority of high-powered policy makers and a majority of powerless backbenchers as Maud (1967) appeared to be recommending is the wrong answer. The elected councillor is the representative of the democratic principle in the world of local government. He is there to check, scrutinize and direct the activities of management, not to be reshaped to fit neatly into a managerial mould.

Since the Maud Report (1967), there has been a welcome degree of criticism of its managerialist assumptions about the councillor's role. Professor Self[31] acknowledges that councillors, being amateurs and part timers, are indeed ill equipped to deal with basic policy-making; but emphasizes that there is much scope for them in the area where policies have their impact on the public. It is the specific case rather than the broad policy that arouses public concern. Their contribution is as often as not to hold a watching brief for a particular public affected by a policy or proposal. And Jeffrey Stanyer[32] has little difficulty in dismissing the notion that systematic selection of councillors is, in any case, feasible. It is not possible to influence parties and electors towards selecting men and women with a set of desired characteristics, or to socialize or train them, once selected, into a certain cast of mind, much less control what they do once on the council. In short, local government can only be 'managerialized' at the expense of politics and representative government. As Self puts it 'An orderly managerial system is inevitably in conflict with the much more erratic and inchoate processes of politics.'[33] Political values cannot be redefined, or political behaviour reshaped, to suit managerial ends.

It was refreshing that when the Bains Committee on management structures for the new local authorities reported in August 1972,[34] they too took a much more relaxed and 'pluralistic' view of councillors' roles than did the earlier Maud Committee. In addition to those who wish to take part in making policy decisions there are, as Bains put it, those who are interested in council membership as a branch of welfare activity, those who wish to serve the community in a general way, those who wish to 'manage' the local authority, often in a rigidly commercial sense, those whose chief aim is to ensure limited spending by the authority. And others. If members' aims are so diverse, why should they all be cast in the one role? They therefore suggested that council members should be encouraged to identify for themselves the area in which they wish to operate. As a corollary they were unhappy with the idea of a hierarchy of importance of functions, with policy-making as the most and constituency work as the least prestigious. Therefore, they argued, policy-making, which involves such key activities as identifying needs, setting objectives, allocating resources, is not something which should be removed from the *general* body of council members.

Nor should an emphasis on policy-making lead to the downgrading of constituency work, making it harder for a member to serve his constituents adequately. Hitherto, members have lacked basic information affecting their areas; members of parties in opposition have had obstacles put in the way of their obtaining information. As Bains points out, the flow of information between elected member and electorate should be a two way process. Members must be informed enough to be able to explain the council's actions and policies to constituents and feed back any reactions to the appropriate quarter.

No formula adequately defines separate spheres of work for 'officials' and 'councillors'. Policy-making, voicing needs and complaints, and exercising democratic control of administration involve the elected members not at some but at all points in the system. There ought not to be any area reserved from their competence. On the other hand, at all points they will encounter, and need, the officials. J. B. Woodham suggests that if we see the authority's activity as ranging from determining long-term objectives, through programme-making and plan-making to execution, there is a syndrome from member control with officer advice and information at the 'objectives' end to officer control with member advice (one might prefer the word 'participation') at the 'execution' end.[35]

This approach sees the local authority less as a *structure* with neatly demarcated components and more as a *network* made up of professional officials and of elected members, each no doubt respecting the special competences of the other, but essentially flexible and capable of constant reshaping as the shape of problems alters.

Officers have a role in helping to stimulate policy; members, as representatives of the consumers of services, have a legitimate interest in their day-to-day administration. In any eufunctioning organization a recognition of spheres of competence will be a naturally occurring thing. An extensive delegation of powers to officers is possible, provided the terms of the delegation are clear and specific, says Bains, and provided also members are capable of constant scrutiny of the administration, and of withdrawal of these powers as and when desirable. *Not* to delegate is, as the Bains Committee points out, to misuse the knowledge and skills of trained officers. On the other hand, they observe that practices hitherto gave members little opportunity to review procedures and monitor progress except when the occasional 'disaster' forced something into the limelight. With the flourishing of managerial and economic techniques it is vital that procedure and performance be constantly scrutinized in the light of aims, and that this be done by people who do not have a vested emotional or professional interest in technical wizardry. Hence the elected member simply as watchdog, as custodian of simple common sense on behalf of consumers, has a more important function in the new managerial world than ever before – if only he can perform it.

The greater acceptability of Bains's approach was attested by one observer's comment that some 62 % of local authorities with a settled management structure by December 1973 appeared to have lifted it straight *from* Bains.[36] This, of course, is a complete negation of the value of flexibility, since each authority's circumstances are different and there ought to be variations between authorities, not uniformity. Nor is Bains without its faults. Some observers have noted its neglect of the party political dimension. The individual councillor's role cannot really be seen without the context of his membership of a political party. Bains is probably unrealistic, for example, in suggesting that opposition parties should have the same help from officials in the way of information as the party in control.

If the Bains approach enables councillors to obtain control of an administrative machine that has often seemed outside democratic control, then it is to be welcomed. Certainly, that is the test by which new forms of internal structure should be judged. *Prima facie*, clearer forms of policy-making ought to contribute to that end. Whether or not they will remains to be seen. J. D. Stewart argues that the Bains structures and processes are not 'anti-political' but that they are the expressions of a management way of putting things. There is a danger of their being part of a mere management movement without a political dimension. The councillor must take control.

Policy must be expressed in the form he seeks and not to meet the requirements of administration . . . The function of management thought in local government should be to assist the political process. The function of political thought on local government should be to give purposive direction to management.[37]

Committees

Local government, even more than most government, is government by committee. The committee is, arguably, the focal point of the councillors' activity and the central instrument of political control. Much discussion of changing local government, therefore, centres on the shape and purposes of the committee structure.

During this century, as local government assumed more and more responsibilities, it tended to become larger and more unwieldy, spawning more and more departments and committees. Formerly council life was concerned less with directions into the future than with the administration of things present, and committees and departments were often independent little worlds of their own, with near monopolies of information about the administration of their services. Since the committee chairman was apt to be its dominant figure (Jones suggests that up to 40 % of all Wolverhampton councillors during the period 1880–1960 made no impact *at all* on council life and work), he tended to run his committee as a petty empire, resenting interference from the rest of the council. 'In 1903 the proceedings of the crucial Finance Committee were described as "a complete farce". You sit round the table and the work is done by the chairman, and the other members say Yes.'[38] The council chamber itself was often a battleground where each chairman sought to promote his own committee's proposals, if necessary at the expense of those of other chairmen. Before 1974 there was a wide variation in practice, from this situation, or where the full council meeting was perhaps merely a formal, rubber stamping exercise, to the other extreme where the full council did everything including receiving and considering the minutes of every single committee and in which individual members could raise any issues they chose.

The latter extreme appears unduly to set aside the efficiencies gained by government by committee; in most cases it would probably only be workable where the role of the political parties was not great or where one party was in overwhelming predominance. The former, 'rubber stamp' model is now equally unacceptable. An excess of power to committees, coupled with the need for overall policy-making, direction and coordination, means that there has to be a powerful central policy-making committee. It would be very easy for this to become unaccountable to anyone but itself. Clearly any such committee must contain most of the key members of the council and would probably be the central instrument whereby the majority party carries out its programme. If efficient policy-making were the be-all and end-all of the local authority no more need be added, save the plenary session rubber stamp. But the council meeting in plenary session is, in a sense, the 'grand forum of the city'. It cannot effectively control every move of the political leadership, and it should not spend its time meticulously wading through every detail of a policy document. But it ought to be a place of debate and criticism on broad policy alternatives, on priorities in resource allocation, a place for flying kites, probing new ideas, and a place for saying things for the national government and press to hear. Several of the new local authorities are governing cities larger than states with seats at the United Nations. Full council is clearly *the* potential focal point for public thinking about principles, priorities and futures.

As to the structure of committees, most authorities in recent years evolved some sort of key committee – whether called a Policy Committee, a Finance and General Purposes Committee or whatever. The Maud Committee (1967) actually suggested a sort of mini-cabinet system; this has not found favour and indeed it would divorce most representatives from policy-making rather than involving them more. This would especially be the case if the body in question were to be made up of members of the majority party only. Nonetheless it remains the case that the new emphasis on policy direction and development necessitates that there be a strong central driving force. With a number of 'programmes' being developed simultaneously, some means is needed of welding them together, evaluating priorities within and between the programmes, allocating resources, and so on. If this is not done an order of priorities will simply emerge out of a process of contest, and the result is likely to be unintended by anyone.

Bains[39] suggested a central Policy and Resources Committee, responsible for the major resources of finance, manpower and land. It would not be the sole arbiter of policy, but it would be able to originate it and make representations to the council on policy matters. This would not be a mini-cabinet; since on balance the Bains Committee considered it advantageous that the minority party be represented on it. This would help to avoid mistrust, massive reversals of policy with swings in electoral fortunes, and a tendency for the officials to find themselves putting the opposition party's case. On the other hand, if it is to be effective and 'efficient', in Bagehot's sense, i.e. a true location of power, this key committee, Bains considered, must reflect the power structure of the major party. The chairman should normally be the leader of the majority party.

Under this central committee Bains suggested four sub-committees, one for each of the three major local resources (finance, land and manpower) and a performance review sub-committee rather on the lines of parliament's Public Accounts Committee, to engage in independent review. Except for their chairmen, the members of these sub-committees would not be members of the parent committee. They would be, in a sense, 'backbenchers', and this would be a means of ensuring for the ordinary 'rank and file' a place in policy-making.

The programmes themselves require committees to oversee them. But two points need to be made. (1) It is stultifying to have a committee merely because there is an administrative department. Indeed it may well be that such an arrangement is a recipe for administrative control over the politician rather than the reverse. Hence the committee structure has to be linked to the overall economic, cultural or physical *objectives* of the authority rather than the provision of specific services which are means to these ends. (2) Representative democracy at local level is not best served if great policy-making power is vested in a committee system so structured as to exclude some representatives from participation. Where the number of committees was reduced during the late 1960s, the Bains Committee found complaints that members were insufficiently occupied. This is of course slightly absurd. There is no reason to refashion a system to accommodate councillors who can only define their usefulness in terms of time spent in committee. Nevertheless the desire of representatives to serve on at least one committee is reasonable. There has been some tendency for younger, brighter councillors to leave on the grounds of their being given no role in effective policy-making.

Maud's most sweeping attack, of course, *was* on the sheer number of committees. It was proposed that most authorities could reduce them from anything upwards of 20 to about 6. This would save time, ensure that administrative trivia should be left to administrators and generally concentrate councillors' minds. Bradford actually managed to achieve 6 (from 25) but in general the reduction was from an average of 21 committees to around 12½. The largest cities had well above 21 committees, but most found Maud's (1967) remedy too drastic. Before Maud (1967), nearly a quarter of all County Borough councillors attended over 50 meetings a year, a proportion which was, it was claimed, greatly reduced by the changes recommended. But almost certainly a good deal of the reduction in committee work was more apparent than real. Greenwood *et al.* quote one town clerk as saying that 'in some towns I am sure that nominal reorganisation has not meant much more than putting a new facade upon a long-standing welter of meetings',[40] while much of the benefit would be negated if the amount of time council members had to spend in each individual meeting were much longer than hitherto, or if more time had to be given to sub-committees and pre-committee caucusing. There has been some suggestion that this often happened.

The big reduction in committees implied, of course, either a substantial number of councillors not sitting on a major committee, or a reduction in the numbers of members of councils. For to reduce committees to say 6 to 8 per council, with a maximum per committee of 15 (the Maud Committee's recommendation), and with at least one committee membership for each councillor, would mean that no authority would need more than 100 elected representatives. Hence in the reorganization under the 1972 Act there was a substantial reduction not only in the numbers of councils but also, per council, of representatives. There is less room for 'backbenchers' in the new system; and far fewer councillors per head of population to perform the humdrum but important job of simply voicing grievances.

Planning by programmes

Until very recently, the internal organization of local government, mirroring its committee structure, was highly departmentalized, inflexible, hierarchical and generally non-innovative in its management style. It was geared to 'administration' within a series of separate areas of activity. It has been to get away from this that increasing attention has been given to the creation of new organizational structures adapted to the interrelatedness of the problems of the cities, capable of 'flexible response' to new situations, and able to serve the new and much needed emphasis on policy planning. Along with this, a range of new techniques of corporate planning have been coming into use. Let us take a brief glimpse at something of what has been happening.

One not untypical case has been that of Liverpool. Having commissioned an inquiry by the McKinsey organization, the city introduced a complete revision of its management structure in December 1969. The idea was to supersede the old departmental structure by 'programme administrations', each under a director, and matching the new council committee structure. These were to deal respectively with Education, Transportation and Basic Services, Housing, Recreation and Open Spaces, Personal Health and Social/Childrens' Services, and Environmental Health and Protection. Secondly there was to be, independently of the 6 programmes, an Administrative Services department and a Land and Property Services department. And finally there was to be a Programme Planning department, chiefly as a staff support to the chief executive, to implement, manage and coordinate the new programme budgeting system, and to do research on management techniques such as measures

113

of impact and performance. Thus the overall concept looked
like this

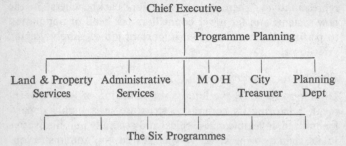

Models such as this have their rationale in an intended shift of
emphasis from the straightforward provision of facilities to
problem analysis and forward planning, coordination, and the
development of new ways of supporting workers in 'the field'.
In the case of the social services, to take one example, this
concept of management links in with the post-Seebohm
reorganization, both being based on the recognition that, to a
substantial extent, needs cannot meaningfully be approached
by one department only. And the work needs the backing of
sophisticated information and diagnosis. Indices of social
malaise indicate that there are very substantial variations from
district to district in the profile of need. Thus, also central to
the concept is the district team consisting of the field workers
of the previously separated departments, the child care officers,
the community development officers, health visitors and so on,
responsible for 'domiciliary support', meals on wheels, home
helps, and for working in coordination with voluntary bodies
for each of a set of divisions of the city.

Certainly the aim of combating departmentalism and
increasing coordination and flexibility of operation is right.
However, often this frenzy of apparent streamlining has something of a 'trendy' air about it. Cutting down the number of
individual labels used is not *per se* a self-evidently valuable
process. Indeed, old inter-departmental problems may simply
be 'buried' from open view inside the new structures. The

Bains Committee found many of the new groupings broadly undesirable. There is little point, they said, in forcing efficiently run departments into illogical groupings in order, for instance, to make one director's work balance with that of another. Further, another layer of management is interposed between the departmental officers and the elected representatives – and indeed the public. Finally, as J. D. Stewart notes, there is the danger that 'far from procedures for coordination being considered first, the organisational change may lead to the illusion that coordination has been achieved'.[41]

The urge towards programme planning and directorates stems from an entirely laudable desire to introduce flexibility and adaptability into the structure of local government. This can be and has been done, however, by effective use of the existing chief officer structure, along the matrix principle. That is to say, by developing alongside the vertical disposition of departments administering services a network of horizontal, cross-department operations. The Chief Executive, for example, would be, as Bains sees it, the leader of a small management team of chief officers. Or there might be a Corporate Planning Group, comprising the deputy heads of all the departments, its work including the identification and review of objectives and priorities, monitoring progress against these.

City managers and chief executives

Another much canvassed concept has been the idea of a single administrative head. The Maud (1967) and Mallaby Committees, with differing emphasis, both recommended that authorities should appoint a Chief Executive Officer or equivalent, who should be the recognized head of the council's paid service, and whose job should be that of coordination and control of departmental work, to ensure consistency with overall objectives.

In many countries, of course, the idea is taken a very great deal further and much local government is conducted by 'managers'. Over a quarter of the population of the USA is governed locally on the 'council-manager' plan, and it is especially to be found in the newer, most rapidly growing cities and suburbs. 'Managers' are also used in Canada, Eire, Scandinavia and Germany. In America the city manager plan originated in an explicit urge to eliminate partisan politics from the local scene. City managers are not only free of 'politics' as partisanship, but they are generally noted for their activist, service-developing outlook, though in part this may be due to the helpful settings in which they work. Cities run by managers have been more ready to accept innovations, and have been on the whole less vulnerable to the particularistic pressures which are such a feature of the life of the bigger, older American cities. However, most managers agree that, like it or not, they *are* political. In a survey, 86 % said they, in effect, led their city councils and were the major policy formulators. The manager is a politician because it is often his role to balance the factors, muster support for policies, draft documents in such a way as to ensure support, and so on. The politics cannot be left out. Here is simply another way of conducting it.

It may be said for the city manager model of urban government that it insulates decision-making from the cruder and more disruptive forms of party politics; that by streamlining the number of those involved it makes purposive action easier; that it makes good use of bureaucracy and expertise. On the other hand it works best in situations where political conflict in the city is not great; where, perhaps, most people are already so satisfied as to really basic needs that they can afford to dispense with the 'gutsier' forms of party politics. In any situation the managerial model is open to the charge of making for a sterile politics in which the concept of a robustly self-governing citizenship has been abandoned yet further.

Although the term 'city manager' was popularly used, the experiment with Mr Frank Harris at Newcastle upon Tyne in the mid 1960s was really rather far from this. As a piece of managerial innovation it was, at best, an instructive failure.[42]

In 1965 Mr Frank Harris was brought from Ford's to be Newcastle's Principal City Officer and the Town Clerk. The latter function was to be secondary, for in the main Harris was to be 'a managing director for town hall business' as he himself put it. He was to coordinate and organize the council's business, ensuring that decisions were speedily implemented, especially with regard to the city's development programme. Harris himself summed up the problem thus, 'Programmes go adrift not through sabotage or inefficiency but because when the ball stops no one knows who should kick it.'[43]

The Harris experiment meant that people were forced to reassess their positions. A great reduction was made in the amount of time councillors spent on non-policy matters. There was a unifying effect on the whole corporation. The innovation was continued after Harris's departure in 1969, though in a modified form. Nonetheless it fell far short of the original hopes that initiated it. The Principal City Officer's role and powers, his relationships with the chief officers and with the city council were never sufficiently spelled out, and, crucially, he lacked sufficient political backing. Councillors resented the apparent shift in power away from them towards officials. In the end, says one commentator, the post came to rely for its efficacy on the personal qualities of its incumbent. This is an example of what may befall managerial innovations undertaken in isolation, without the thinking through of the implications for the existing system of powers and responsibilities.

The Bains Committee found there was little support for the concept of an all-powerful Chief Executive. By the time of reorganization, however, most of the larger authorities had evolved a post of head of administration. Although the name might be retained, the new post did not bear more than a superficial resemblance to the traditional, mainly legal, concept of a Town Clerk. The job was principally the leadership of the chief officers as a team, and the ensuring of effective use of organization and resources. Bains felt that, while it might have its own small staff of aides, the post should not have a 'department' of its own to compete, and be involved in rivalries, with service departments.[44]

In another recent development teams of chief officers, under the chairmanship of the chief executive officer, have been working together on such tasks as monitoring the progress of projects, especially those which represent new departures in policy and tendering collective advice. In Nottingham, for instance, the Chief Officers Group under the Chief Executive Officer consisted of the treasurer, engineer, estates surveyor, architect, planning officer, housing manager and director of education. It considered policy to be recommended to the council on (a) matters affecting separate departments, (b) important development schemes and (c) action to implement the council's policies over such matters as development schemes.

Its main contribution, according to Greenwood *et al.*, was towards the building up of a comprehensive picture of what the council was planning in the field of building and other engineering construction. They comment that

It may well be that the Nottingham pattern with its stress on the chief executive officer's role as leader of a chief officers group and also with its emphasis on the need for coordinated policy planning as well as implementation may show the future line of development of the chief executive officer.[45]

Efficiency – for What?

New managerial techniques are now coming into use, the objects of which are to indicate the needs which must be met by the local authority and the several alternatives, with their attendant costs, that might be pursued in answering them.[46] They are an attempt to provide the tools whereby city governments may make decisions about future policies, helping thus to ensure that the future is approached by conscious options rather than drifted into willy nilly. In theory, this is fine. In the case of some of the more ambitious techniques, however, it needs to be asked whether there is not a likelihood of the aspiration being taken for the substance. How possible is this kind of corporate planning in the real world? How compatible is it with some of the other values which we might wish to promote or preserve? Let us look briefly at two of these techniques, the Planning Programming Budgeting System (PPBS) and the land-use transportation study (LTS).

The objective of PPBS is to identify and examine the goals to be pursued in each major area of governmental responsibility; to formulate specific future objectives, for which different alternative methods of attainment are evaluated, for cost, effectiveness, and impacts on other valued ends, including other objectives of the same authority. The questions asked of any particular aspect of governmental work are, why is this activity undertaken? What is the right objective? Are there other ways of doing it? Ultimately a decision has to be reached and a programme adopted. The land-use transportation survey is an attempt to follow a similar procedure in respect to the relationship between the changing pattern of transport facilities, both public and private, and the uses of land which change in relation to it. The provision of a motorway or rapid rail system may have a profound effect on residential preferences and land values in the hinterland of a big city; conversely, developments in urbanization will create transportation needs. Hence the folly of attempting to provide for either in isolation from the other, as has happened in the past. The land-use transportation study begins with the collection of the best available information on future probable population, changing industrial and occupational structure, land uses, future priorities and requirements, etc., and then examines the consequence for land use and transport of different potential lines of future urban development. These might include finger development out from the existing urban area using existing, improved, and new transport networks; outward spread of the existing area close to its own present borders; or 'blobs' of development dispersed throughout the hinterland, using existing urbanized centres as cores; or combinations of all three.

In either of these exercises the central purpose is to impel all concerned in running the city to think about the objectives to which they should be working, to facilitate scrutiny of existing operations in the light of those objectives, and to bring as much information and argument as possible to bear on alternative courses of future action. The main benefits lie in the hope of escaping from the dominance of the week by week minutiae of administration, and of initiating and facilitating debate on ends and means, values, strategy and tactics, benefits in relation to costs, and so on.

Debate about social issues is indeed vitiated by lack of clarity concerning the values implicit in different types of activity and the costs which the maintenance of these values imposes on the community. One of the most obvious examples is the cost of private motoring versus public transport. But in every area examples abound. How do we weigh the social and human costs of certain types of housing against economies in monetary terms or land? How much value in terms of other costs borne do we place on not building on green belts? In housing schemes how much are we prepared to pay, per person housed, for 'x' amount of better environment? Anything that exposes these questions, that demands an answer from us, should help us make better decisions.

However, the danger with planning and budgeting systems and similar techniques is that the system itself may take over. The tasks of serving the 'programme' may become more resource consuming than could possibly be justified by the resulting output of policy analysis. It may obfuscate rather than illuminate, by encouraging the gathering of unhelpful data, and by calling attention to *itself* rather than its objectives. The existence of a mechanism for planning is not the same as actually planning; but it is all too easy for it to cause the activity itself to recede further and further into the background. Data collection is not an end in itself. Instead of achieving clarity of purpose, there is the possibility of policies being cobbled together along the lines that *seem* to be indicated by the available data. The history of airport siting decisions might be taken to illustrate this.

By no means everything is quantifiable. Many things on which people would place a high value are not only impossible to express in quantifiable terms, such as financial, but even may be *cheapened* by any such attempt. At the same time, central to these approaches is the belief that everything that *can* be expressed in concrete, or quantifiable terms, should be.

It requires considerable skill and willpower not to let what cannot be quantified be dominated by what can. Conflicts may well emerge between bureaucrats defending what a computer has indicated, and citizens objecting in the name of some value not subject to quantification. One partial solution is to include in the analysis not only economic, demographic and similar measurables but also, via surveys, some fairly strong indicators of affected people's own preferences. This is likely to work best on highly specific proposals in which people have a close personal involvement – such as the environmental quality of a housing scheme or the location of a proposed runway or roadway. But the less specific the impact of the issue on particular citizens the less is this likely to be of use. In neither case is the decision-maker relieved of the responsibility to decide; including in his decision the weighing of factors and values which have little information to back them along with those which have much.

PPBS, cost-benefit analysis, LTS, etc. may seem like the ultimate triumph of managerial and research technology over politics, and, that indeed is what they could become. But they must not. J. D. Stewart quotes a leading US specialist, who says 'In one sense PPB can be viewed as introducing a new set of participants into the decision process, which . . . I have labelled partisan efficiency advocates.'[47] We are back once more at the question 'efficiency for what'? And at the need for people in city government who can ask it persistently and tenaciously.

Corporate planning, therefore, is a management movement laden with political implications. It will have failed democracy if it becomes a means of deodorizing city government, of taking the politics out, instead of enhancing 'the richness and complexities of policies'.[48]

Conclusion

With all these changes we have, then, far fewer elected representatives, working in far larger authorities, with far more sophisticated management techniques. The irony of it is that each step forward along these lines takes local government further away from the set of conditions which justified it in the nineteenth century. Intimacy with local conditions has always been one of the chief justifications of local government. John Stuart Mill wrote in his classic account in *Representative Government*, that

If the local authorities and public are inferior to the central ones in knowledge of the principles of administration, they have the compensating advantage of a far more direct interest in the results.[49]

Hence the pull towards larger, remoter units, towards pre-occupations with long term, large scale planning, ought to be counterbalanced by a pull in the other direction, towards those with a 'direct interest in the result'. One possibility, canvassed by Professor Self,[50] is for grafting on to local (or regional) government separate representative bodies for each principal public service, such as education or planning, which would participate in their administration, though without having spending powers. We might call this a 'vertical' solution. The possibilities of a 'horizontal' one, bringing in the neighbourhoods at the receiving end of the services, are discussed in a later chapter. Such proposals might help to strengthen the consumer's end of the urban governmental process. Whatever their objectives, the recent developments have increased the power, sophistication and in many cases the remoteness of our city governments. Anything would be welcome which increased their openness to the test of public scrutiny.

Preoccupation with structural reform can easily displace allegiance to the purposes the organization is there to serve. We need, now, to focus attention and debate in the field of city government on the policies themselves, the quality of policy-making and the impact of policies on people. It is in the light of these that the wisdom or folly of the changes of the late 1960s and early 1970s will ultimately be judged.

Chapter 2 Raising the Revenue

Money is power and cities need it. But everywhere, not just in Britain, cities 'seem to be subject to an iron law of poverty',[1] with resources inadequate to their needs and aspirations. This raises at once for us two questions. Do present methods of funding city government produce enough money to meet our needs? Are present methods fair and effective? To both questions, grave doubts are being increasingly heard. And there is a third question. In Britain, as in most countries, cities are heavily dependent upon the central government for their revenue. Can there be any real local autonomy when Whitehall so substantially pays the piper?

On the latter question, Professor Marshall argues that if local democracy is to have any meaning, local authorities must have a degree of autonomy in respect of the scale and type of their activities. However, 'increasing dependence on the national exchequer is making this difficult to achieve'.[2] There has been a rising curve of dependence on central government as the proportion of locally raised to centrally distributed money has decreased. In 1965–6 the percentage of net expenditure raised from central government grants was 55 %. By the early 1970s it was around 60 %. The rates raised 48 % of local authority revenue in 1891. This proportion has been almost halved. We have a constantly mounting level of expectations in all fields, especially in the 'big spenders', housing and education, combined with an understandable reluctance on the part of local politicians to increase the sums raised locally through the rates even to the level of annually keeping pace with inflation, let alone to providing for new and expanded activities. Local authorities already spend 15 % of the GNP, and we can expect this proportion to get greater (of recent years indeed, their spending has been growing faster than the GNP). If the trend continues for the centre to provide the bulk of this, we can expect further stiflings of the grounds of local initiative, runs one common complaint.

The justification for increasing locally raised revenues rests simply, then, on two premises. Firstly, that there is a rising curve of expenditure which, under present arrangements, can only otherwise be met by increasing dependence on the central government. As Marshall puts it 'The local level should not have to be compelled to live in perpetual fear of a centralising vortex.'[3] Secondly, the desire for greater devolution and citizen participation in a more robustly democratic local government system hardly seems compatible with central government handouts providing the overwhelming bulk of the finance available.

Much of this lamentation is based, however, on presupposition and not evidence. It is unlikely that there *is* a direct correlation between financial dependence on central government and the strangulation at birth of local initiative. Boaden[4] has shown the existence of very great variation in the expenditure patterns and policy initiatives of English county boroughs, and that, in explaining these, the 'needs' of an area and the political dispositions of its council have been key factors, financial resources being more of a constraining factor on these than an active factor in its own right. Central control tends to be alleged to be a self evident consequence of the proportion of local revenue coming from the centre. There would have to be proof that it is *necessarily* an inhibiting factor beyond that which *any* unitary system of parliamentary government would be bound to exercise *vis-à-vis* subordinate bodies. Demands for national standards of service provision may have as much, if not more, to do with government control as the growth of grant aid itself.

Again, another commentator has suggested that respect for local autonomy by the centre may be the essential precondition of its letting local authorities use part of the tax field the centre at present holds, and that the possession of local taxes may be the consequence rather than the cause of improved status on the part of the cities.[5]

In the absence, therefore, of detailed investigation into this aspect of central-local relations, there has been much room for thinly grounded argument.

The bulk of city expenditures goes on obligatory functions – i.e. duties and services for which the city is administering a national requirement. The area for expansion of local finance without recourse to central sanction is not large. Central government will probably prove, when it comes to the crunch, reluctant to yield control of sources of revenue which at present it enjoys. However the money is raised or spent, government control of the national economy would be made nonsense of, if so large a source of public expenditure were even partially free to develop in its own way.

Moreover, greater autonomy to the cities would almost certainly intensify disparities between different areas in resources *vis-à-vis* social needs. National control, with a rate support grant system, does at least go some way towards territorial justice (the matching of resources to needs) than would otherwise be the case. Further, any increase in local taxing powers, particularly over items of local consumption, would be likely to increase the pressures on local politicians to keep taxes down at the possible expense of service provision. In revenue terms, local autonomy could be tantamount to a tax on the poorer areas and a bonus for the rich. It could present the disadvantaged with the freedom to go to the wall. As Professor Marshall observes, 'a populace with a keen sense of justice, observing local government's unequal efforts, and interpreting "fair shares" as meaning uniform services from Lands End to John O' Groats, is apt to look to ministers rather than to councillors'.[6]

The 'democratic' case for increasing the local contribution to expenditure is, therefore, not quite as clear cut as it would seem. In fact, whether the citizen would benefit in terms of better service provision would probably continue to depend, as it does now, on the particular services affecting him and the policies respecting them that central government and his particular local government have adopted.

The system of local government financing hitherto in use is, however, widely held, with reason, to be unsatisfactory. On the central government side, what proportion of national expenditure is to be allocated for local services is a matter of national priorities and national politics. But the structure of the central payments system can introduce only partially intended, if intended at all, biases into local government (as in the case of urban roads schemes). The formula for determining the rate support grant is a blunt instrument, the effect of which is that revenues often do not go to the authorities which have incurred the most expenditure.[7] At the local government level, it is increasingly doubted whether the rating system is adequate or equitable. And this is not just a technical matter, for it is at least as important to the citizen's view of 'democracy' in local government that local revenue should be seen to be raised rationally and fairly as that there should be 'x' degree of fiscal autonomy *vis-à-vis* Westminster.

The pros and cons of the existing rating system illustrate the difficulties facing any proposal for change. In some respects it is an inequitable method of revenue raising. Rating is essentially a tax on residence rather than income. However, 'the rental value of a home does not necessarily vary in proportion to the occupant's ability to pay'.[8] The rate rebate, of course, is designed for this, but a system needing to hand money back, in effect, to a large group of otherwise financially able citizens cannot be sound. Rates also have the disadvantage of raising extremely variable yields from one place to another, much more so than many other possible forms of taxation. The distribution of car usage, for example, is more evenly spread across the country than that of rental values. The result is that the rates have yielded as much as 60 % of the income of some councils and as little as 10 % of that of others. At times of rapid inflation, the erosion of real yield over a year embarrasses the local authority severely. Rating is often said to be cheap and easy to administer, but this argument ignores the complexity and upheaval of revaluation.

Rates now account for about 25 % of local authority revenue. Any alternative, therefore, must produce at least a comparable proportion if it is not to increase dependence on central government. The RIPA* have urged, also,[9] that the subject of the alternative should be widely distributed over the country, that the levy should be variable at the local authority's discretion, and that it should not be too expensive to run. There would be some gain, too, for citizen involvement in local affairs if citizens could see some connection between what they pay and the activities of their local authority. It must not, to be realistic, be a tax which the government itself might want to use as a regulator of the economy, such as a local purchase tax – and it must not encroach on the government's overall capacity to run the economy. It must be a 'good tax', i.e. convenient to administer, difficult to evade, clear in application. Finally, in a situation where several tiers of government are entitled to spend citizens' money, it must be clear which authority is entitled to which revenues.

The RIPA working party (1956) argued for (i) a local income tax on personal incomes with equivalent charges on companies, (ii) a local entertainments tax to replace central government duties, and (iii) motor vehicle duties and driving licence fees to be transferred to the local authority. Of these the case for the last was the least strong, while only the first, of all taxes, offered a prospect of a long term solution to local authority revenue problems.

'Those who would argue in favour of a change in the system are faced by an unhealthy coalition of politicians and bureaucrats.'[10] Yet the main canvassed alternatives have been tried and tested in other countries, and the evidence of their effective use is there to see.

In Finland and Sweden there is a local income tax, which helps to explain the high degree of financial independence local authorities there enjoy. It is also in use in the US as a means of

* Royal Institute of Public Administration.

taxing the 'bedroom suburbs' for their use of central city facilities. Local income tax would be more equitable and more flexible than the rates. Income tax is *the* tax which allows, straightforwardly, for differences in capacity to pay. Some people who at present pay no direct local tax, such as lodgers, would be brought into line with everyone else. It is relatively simple to administer in that the basic assessment work will already have been done for national purposes. Moreover, only a local income tax is a large and comprehensive enough potential revenue source to bear comparison with the rates. In Sweden local income tax amounts to a third of the money raised in *all* forms of taxation and pays for fuel and power, medical services and transport services. It is however, centrally, not locally, assessed and collected. In Britain central admini-stration would help preserve a valued principle – the con-fidentiality of one's income tax return. On the other hand, this would lead to local being fixed to *national* income tax and hence central government would retain considerable, some would say excessive, power to fix the rate. A report for the Royal Institute of Public Administration suggested in 1968 that the rate of tax should be fixed by the local authority subject to limits prescribed by law. The Municipal Treasurers,* however, have suggested that it should be deducted from national income tax.[11]

The disadvantage of local income tax is that it would not give those authorities with substantial inner city demands the kind of tax base they need. Considering inner London's financial needs, however, R. Kirwan[12] urges a local income tax for the whole of the metropolitan area, so organized that the poorer boroughs would have access to the resources of the richer.

Sales taxes are much used in the USA. But they are a tax on living standards, they are regressive and are subject to fluctua-tions in yield. Quite apart from the existence of VAT already, central government prefers to keep its eyes on this sector as a possible economic regulator.

* The Institute of Municipal Treasurers and Accountants.

It would be easy to allocate some of the taxes at present levied by central government to the disposal of local government – such as entertainment taxes, motor licence duties or petrol taxes; though such a move would be fraught with political difficulties. A local authority might find itself under irresistible pressure to lower existing rates of tax; so it might still be desirable to have a central body retaining the power to fix tax levels. As with sales taxes, it might be argued that some of these would bring in such a small sum that they would be more of an irritant than an aid. Petrol taxes were at one time considered a possible additional source. They would after all be a direct tax on road congesters, noise and air polluters. Under the new local boundary structure, the possibility of avoidance by buying petrol in an adjacent, cheaper area has been much reduced. Since October 1973, however, this option has probably become politically unacceptable. Nevertheless, if taxes on motor fuel, driver's licences and vehicle licences (which together bring in over £300 million p.a.) *were* removed to the local authorities the RIPA estimate a reduction on exchequer dependence from well over half of present revenue to about a quarter. Professor Marshall agrees, 'There is no gain and a good deal of harm to local autonomy in the central collection and filtering back through the grant mechanism of monies which the local authorities could well collect themselves.'[13]

None of these schemes does more than increase, or transfer to the local authorities, the funds available from present known sources. There are two further possibilities. Firstly, to 'hive off' to market forces certain of the services at present provided by the community but which could be financed by the individual consumer. Maynard and King argue this strongly in economic terms.[14] It would still be necessary, they acknowledge, for needy private individuals to be publicly helped. At one logical extreme this argument entails the decimation of both rates and government grants. The contribution of user charges should not be ignored; but unless we are prepared to contemplate the dismantling of the public machinery for coping with the needs and the ills of urban life which has been so long and painfully built up, this thinking is of little value. Secondly, there may be scope for local initiative in new and hitherto untried directions. In terms of the overall picture these might be financially marginal, but if tied to the raising of money for specific local projects – such as building a new swimming pool or public hall – might be of added appeal and successfully 'top up' existing resources. For example, an attempt has been made to introduce a measure allowing local authorities to hold lotteries without the need for further parliamentary sanction.

Only some form of local income tax could be a substitute for the rates, but these other proposals could help either to reduce local dependence on central grants, or provide wider local flexibility, and hopefully both.

Education accounts for about half the local budget. There is a case here for easing the local burden by transferring *away* from the local authority to the Exchequer the payment of the teachers, and that of the police. Their incomes are negotiated and fixed nationally in any case, and it is not obvious that the removal from the local budget of the 30 % of it taken up by these wages and salaries would make any difference to the scope of local initiative.

The Conservative government's Green Paper[15] on the future of local government finance (July 1971) argued the objections to each potential change with considerable force. It appeared to set aside the evidence accumulated by the IMTA, the RIPA and others. It did however point to ways of making the rating system more equitable (by having valuations relate to the capital rather than the rental value of a property); and it proposed altering the grants system to enable each local authority to provide a standard level of service for a standard amount per head. (In 1974 the Conservatives announced their conversion to the abolition of rates – though without making clear what would replace them.)

The finding of sufficient capital, from *whatever* source, to provide for the cities' needs and particularly for investment in the inner and poorer areas must take priority over the shifting of the central–local balance. But the two are not incompatible.

The begging bowl approach of local to central government is satisfactory neither for local democracy nor for the prospects of effective action in the poorer areas. Movement to change this outworn system at last looks like bearing fruit. The Association of Municipal Corporations has long urged a Royal Commission to be set up within a few years of reorganization; while the 1974 Labour government set up the Layfield Committee, to report in 1975.[16] There is increasing consensus on the need for change; the substance thereof could be as profound in its effects on urban government and urban problems as any change we have seen so far. Whatever is done, will be no panacea, however; for 'the long term prospect for urban areas generally is still likely to be of a continuing rapid increase in the demand for expenditure and hence of a continuing problem of obtaining finance'.[17]

Part Four **The Functionary Élite and Planning**

Chapter 1 Townscape with Bureaucrats: and Matters Arising

> *There could not be a moment's hesitation between representative government, among a people in any degree ripe for it, and the most perfect imaginable bureaucracy. But it is, at the same time, one of the most important ends of political institutions, to obtain as many of the qualities of the one as are consistent with the other...*
> – J. S. Mill[1]

> *Today the enemy of human freedom is the managerial society and the central coercive power which goes with it ...*
> – R. H. S. Crossman[2]

The central fact of urban government in Britain in this century is its increasing bureaucratization.

Until quite recently, in British public debate there seemed little room for argument that expressed concern over some of the implications of government by bureaucracy while at the same time declining to translate this into a defence of private enterprise and small government. In the last decade, however, the situation has altered dramatically, for a wide range of argument has been opened up in just this area. It is, however, a somewhat inchoate debate, since if the free market is in many fields an unacceptable alternative to government by bureaucracy, the latter's new critics are not putting forward any other clear-cut alternative model. Most of the most fruitful criticism has dealt with means of making governmental bureaucracy more responsive and sensitive, rather than replacing it altogether.

This is only realistic, for bureaucracy and the modern liberal democratic state go hand in hand.

The impetus towards the continued growth of bureaucratic government comes from two sources. Firstly, the development of a range of governmental activities in fields such as social provision, which it is widely felt cannot effectively or fairly be provided by the free market. Secondly, along with this, the belief that governmental coordination, regulation and forward planning is technically superior to, more efficient than, private competition. Both elements are present, for example, in the Labour Party's attitude to nationalization. And both contribute to the rationale of planning.

Theoretically, the use of bureaucratic organization in any field may be justified as the embodiment of rationality. That is to say, it is methodical, operates according to conclusions drawn from observable evidence, and so on. No one expects it to work perfectly, of course; the evidence may be partial or misleading, the theory faulty. But governmental bureaucracy is different from other forms of bureaucracy. Its products are not, on the whole, subject to the disciplines of the market-place. The consumers, that is the public, are not free to take or leave; on the contrary, governments can, in the last resort, use substantial coercive powers against recalcitrant members of the public. Hence the problem of the exercise of control by elected representatives is crucial.

Ideally, the system operates on the premiss that politicians can and do exercise control. In practice, however, there are formidable reasons why, often, they do not.

The greatest feature of a permanent corps of officials in government is not, as some seem to think, the social background they come from; nor yet, though it is nearer to the mark, that they engage in what is popularly thought of as 'bureaucracy'; but that they represent a corpus of experience and information usually far outweighing that available to anyone else. Put pessimistically, such is their apparent expertise that an outside critic, to be effective, has to be an expert himself. What Piet Thoenies calls 'the functionary élite' possess

the insight required for the interpretation of factors; by carrying out such interpretation they increase the insight; they are then capable of taking a still more subtle attitude, seek still more abtruse information, get hold of still more expertly drawn up reports, and become still more expert themselves.[3]

Ultimately, only those of adequate technical standing can properly judge what they do. (It should not be inferred that the functionary élite of professionals and officials necessarily *want* to use their expertise to take political decisions. Generally, it is reasonable to assume that civil servants prefer firm political direction *when they can get it*.)

When elected representatives, especially the amateur ones of local government, are called on to make choices, many of the criteria for evaluating the proposals of officials are provided by those officials themselves. And as Louis Altschuler puts it, 'Politicians cannot evaluate every argument presented by an administrative official. They must therefore assess the competence of men and professions, and not, in most instances, arguments.'[4] The technical arguments underlying proposals may well tend to pre-empt the decision to be taken. For example, a citizen, or councillor even, tries to argue about a plan for a road development produced by an engineer. There is here firstly, an imbalance between a non-expert and an expert. There is likely secondly to be an imbalance in the quality of argument, perhaps between hard data and non-measurable values. The road plan can be supported by a plethora of evidence, financial, geological and social (such as traffic flow statistics). In many circumstances it might be said that the decision to have as environmental supremo a planner, or a traffic engineer, or any other species of expert, could be *the* really major decision in that field taken by a city council, for its consequence could be that in future decision-making the main weight of priority was already determined. This would be an extreme reading of the case, and one which excessively underrates the politician's role. Nevertheless, there is no reason to exempt Britain from Prof. Walsh's comment that generally, 'it is the planners, rather than the politicians and community groups, who are thinking about the directions in which the metropolis should grow, about desirable standards for education, housing and community services, and about the future of urban society'.[5]

This leads us to consider one of the concomitants of bureaucratization – that of professionalization. The two are not the same thing, and the problems they pose for political control are not identical. Professionalization involves the increasing use of experts who have been specially trained to the mastery of a specific discipline, specific knowledge and specific techniques, and whose claim to authority rests not only in the official positions of which they are incumbents but also in their standing as members of a national and international group of similarly trained people having substantial control over criteria for membership and subsequent behaviour. If a city government recruits professionals it has decided, in effect, to devote resources to acquiring and using a corpus of specialized knowledge whose ultimate source and point of reference is not specific to the city. To a degree, 'professionals' are cosmopolitans in a local world. They may enjoy prestige to the extent that the city needs their services rather than they its employment, i.e. to the extent that they can, if frustrated in their aims, pack up and take their scarce skills elsewhere. Moreover, one of the key characteristics of a profession is its relative autonomy in defining what it is about. Its members are subject to professional values (and fashions) and their success in conforming to these may be more valuable to them in career terms than how they accomplish their tasks as defined by their clientele. Bluntly, the serving of one's client badly might be less damaging to a professional's prospects than to be stuck with an out of date notion.

Professionals in public service are, then, professionals in a unique position. They are pulled by the claims of their profession to define standards in a way which, in effect, makes a claim to autonomy of operation, while working in a sphere in which, in theory, they are officials under orders from a political, i.e. lay, directorate.

Where, as in the case of lawyers or engineers, well-defined professional values and standards are of long-standing and nationally recognized, this is probably not much of a problem. But a number of positions in the urban government scene are tenanted by people whose professional position is far from established and well defined. This is, for example, the case with planners. Not only do people in planning come to it from a heterodox background, with qualifications that might be in sociology, geography, economics, architecture, engineering and perhaps others, but no settled opinion, one might suggest, has yet emerged as to what the scope and limits of planning are. Planners, says Altschuler, 'can hardly judge themselves except by their ability to present material in a handsome format, their knowledge of planning fashions, and their immediate potential success'.[6]

Although bureaucratic procedure is aimed at the elimination of uncertainties, there is always bound to be a certain ineradicable degree of uncertainty. A claim to rationality and efficiency can only be subject to the limitations of available resources of time, money, manpower and information. And the more the activity concerns future planning, the more does the unknowability of the future, which makes fools of us all, make grandiose claims, on the part of bureaucrats and professionals, foolish. Hitherto it has not been a noted characteristic of bureaucracies to advertise the limitations to which their thinking is subject.

Yet one of the most noted features of bureaucratic organization is that once an idea has been floated, it can acquire almost an autonomous life of its own. For example, once some actor in a situation decides to support an idea, he has, in effect, made an investment in it, an investment of his own prestige. It may be difficult for him to withdraw it without loss. And he will be reluctant to see his 'capital' diminish through the actions of others. Others, seeing this investment, may make theirs accordingly, judging the idea not only on its merits but also, perhaps even largely, in the light of the supports it has gathered. When, therefore, someone is strongly committed to a proposal, he will be likely to seek to commit others to it also, and to resist moves to defeat it, unless and until the costs of persisting in his investment outweigh the benefits.[7]

Anthony Downs[8] hypothesizes that whenever there is great pressure upon a bureau to make a decision quickly, then (i) a minimum number of alternatives will be considered; (ii) primary consideration will be given to those prepared in advance and 'ready to go'; (iii) decision-makers will try to restrict the numbers of people participating, and the diversity of their views, as much as possible; (iv) if possible, secrecy will be used to restrict participation. It is a matter of judgement what constitutes pressure to make a decision quickly, of course. The pressure is always present to some degree. Similar effects are likely to arise from the imperative not to waste resources of time, money and manpower in procedures which might result in the prevention or postponement of a decision deemed necessary. And once a decision has been taken, there will be great pressure on the bureau to prevent the issue from being reopened.

It is hard to deny officials the same measure of self-interest that the rest of us are wont to claim. It is only human for a department not to want to undo a programme on which it has worked for years, for instance, at the behest of a new and perhaps inexperienced team of political masters. It may be its duty to warn politicians against embarking on policies tried before and found unworkable. Yet clearly the line between this legitimate activity and the usurpation of the role of elected representatives is very thin. The British civil servant's traditional sense of administrative responsibility may not be of much use as a guideline in many of the fields of activity developed in urban government since the war.[9]

Elsewhere in this part of the book planning is taken as the example of the bureaucratic/professional phenomenon. *Mutatis mutandis*, however, we could have taken other fields, such as education or the social services. The citizen faces analogous problems here; though the prospect for alteration of the relationship may be more promising.

Why should the admittedly necessary growth of the bureaucratic/professional machinery of urban government be a cause for concern? Because its potential for power is very considerable and our potential for surveillance and control over it is uncertain. Because, as Robert Nisbet puts it, 'by its very triumph of rationality, scientific administration has reduced much of the elbow room, much of the intellectual and moral friction, which ethical individuality must have if it is to flourish'.[10] Because, *pace* Nisbet, much that goes on in the guise of rationality is, in practice, anything but. Because the claims of the public dimension, of democratic citizenship, entail that value choices and commitments be made publicly by public men and not wrapped up as matters of value-neutral technique or administration. Because great power over the definition of the situation rests with those in government over against the public, and not least with those who have been called in to occupy permanent paid positions.

The line between acknowledgement of the authority of government as legitimate, and uncritical acceptance of its activities as benevolently and competently conducted, is not a clear one, and it often suits those in authoritative positions to see that it is kept hazy. Yet there are signs that we are in a crisis of authority, with a wave of sentiment against politics, against the taking of large decisions, against planning, against the use of expertise at the very time when all of these are, if anything, more needed than ever. How, then, can we reconcile the unavoidable fact that the way we live now entails government by bureaucrats and professionals, with the legitimate claims of citizenship and democracy? Looked at from one perspective, this is an old problem in a new guise; and the name of the problem is, authority. We must return to it.

Chapter 2 Bureaucratic Offensives in the Guise of Planning: Two Cases

Planning that dispenses with the autonomous, traditional values of a population can be effectuated only by a system of administration that is eventually forced to liquidate these values. For these will then constitute forces of distraction, even of subversion, to the abstract ends of planning.
– Robert A. Nisbet[1]

You will be aware that the houses in the above area must be demolished as soon as possible because they are unfit to live in. To enable demolition to take place the Housing and Estates Manager has made you two offers of alternative suitable accommodation which I understand have been refused by you. I hereby give you notice that the offer will remain open for acceptance by you until—, and if you do not accept by that date, no more offers of accommodation will be made and steps will be taken, without further notice to you, to have you evicted from the property . . .
– Letter to a 77-year-old Sunderland widow[2]

All that glisters is not gold, and not all that is done in the name of planning is necessarily planning. What is, depends upon the definition of planning adopted. In one sense, planning as a term might be restricted to what emanates from planning departments. In another, it is part of the technical armoury of modern management. In another, looser sense, it is often applied very widely to the outputs of government departments in general. The same confusion applies to the term 'planner', which can apply to almost any official, or to someone recognized as qualified by the Town Planning Institute. And even if we were to accept one definition to work with, there would still be bad planning, planning compromised by non-planning pressures and considerations, and so on. All of this, before we got on to the question of what might constitute 'good' planning.

This is a necessary preliminary to the consideration of what has, in practice, been done in the name of planning. From the point of view of the citizens affected, however, the result is what matters, not the version of 'planning' that has brought it about. Of the two cases examined subsequently, the first is about planning in the looser sense of the activities of local government officials, here chiefly housing officials, while the second deals with 'planning' on an altogether grander plane of pretension. The charge levelled is broadly the same: bureaucratic aggression against defenceless citizens.

Slum clearance, Sunderland style

If ever there was an idea whose time had come, it was the idea of slum clearance in the last quarter century. The universal acceptance of it meant that, after the war, we created large and powerful organizations whose main justification was to remove slums. This stemmed from a generous and urgent impulse towards the liberation of all from the evils of bad housing. (Because the tools of liberation in the twentieth century are often bureaucratic, it is easy to forget the ends for which they were fashioned.) In recent years however, it has become increasingly clear that, as the very worst parts of our housing stock become cleared, there are often no very objective criteria for proceeding further; but we are left with, in each city, a bureaucratic-cum-political machine which has that most dangerous of properties – an existence that needs justification. Slum clearance has been that justification.

It is reasonable to assume that the bulk of housing replacement activity undertaken up to the late 1950s was aimed at the clearance of housing conditions which were by any standard, intolerably foul, decayed and so deficient in amenities as to constitute a menace to the physical and mental well-being of those who had to live there. It is also reasonable to assume that these conditions were, in most cases, such that no measure

143

short of whole-scale demolition would suffice. It was patently unfair and untrue to attach to these areas and people the designation 'slums' and 'slum-dwellers'. Yet it was a term which had a multiplicity of handy social uses. It satisfied the urge to stigmatize. It could imply both social distance and detachment. It was particularly of appeal to the liberal. The term could urge his conscience to social action while not necessarily depriving him of the psychological gratifications of its other uses. And since it had no precise meaning, anyone could use it at will and without much prospect of contradiction. It was, in short, a very useful term indeed.

By the late 1950s, in many places the programmes of clearance of the very worst housing were nearing completion. The question then began to arise, by what criteria and according to whose judgement, should the municipal bulldozer continue to roll?

The studies undertaken in Sunderland by Norman Dennis[3] catch the clearance process just at this point where, for increasing numbers of citizens, the rehousing machine is turning from a beneficent if blunt instrument, into a bureaucratic juggernaut.

How, for example, did the officials of Sunderland go about deciding which areas to include in the 1960–65 clearance scheme? New areas were selected on the basis of somewhat random evidence – the 'personal knowledge' of district inspectors, complaints of tenants anxious to bring pressure on their landlords, requests for sanitary inspection by people wanting to gain points for the council-housing list, and so on. Next, 'all dwellings in prospective slum clearance areas were then examined to enable particular decisions to be made about their fitness for human habitation. According to a public health inspector the investigation of each dwelling during this exercise took about two minutes.'[4] Compulsory purchase orders were then applied for in respect of the condemned areas. The public inquiry that ensued was concerned mainly with objections from owner occupiers dissatisfied with the amount of compensation.

There were undoubtedly, clear grounds for many of the

condemnations. Defects of structure were reported in 65 % of cases. Only 5 % of respondents to a survey said there had been any major modernization by the landlord since they had become tenants. A majority, 57 % of the families, were in favour of demolition, 42 % very much so. Residents wanting a change to council housing looked forward to better internal facilities – fixed baths and piped hot water. However, each figure 'has as its complement the responses of those people who feared that in one way or another they would find they had suffered rather than gained by rehousing'.[5] These people feared the loss of the advantages of nearness to the town centre, good neighbours and cheap housing (they feared the cost of council rents). Although, therefore, a majority of the families in 1960–65 favoured council demolition policy, 43 % were actually *opposed* to demolition, and 23 % considered they would be *very much worse off* in a council estate as compared with their present area.

In short, a substantial number of houses due for demolition were considered by their inhabitants to provide a satisfactory, and often well-loved environment. Even if some of these should turn out to be demonstrably dangerous to health, whatever their inhabitants might think, the question was beginning to arise whether council clearances were based on adequate justification. Compulsory powers were beginning to be used, *against* their supposed beneficiaries – the people were being forced to be free, whether they would or no.

The bulk of proposals for 1965–70 continued to concern housing clearly deficient in both structure and amenity. In Sunderland in the housing proposed for demolition in 1965–70, 82 % of a sample still lacked an indoor toilet, and 66 % had no fixed bath. Many people felt their district to be unattractive because of the proximity of noxious industry. The presence of children in a family enhanced greatly the sense of dissatisfaction with housing conditions. In all, 28 % of those living in the areas to be cleared expressed dissatisfaction, in one particular district the proportion rose to 50 %. In this latter area 57 % thought they would be better off in a council house and 33 % of families had in fact applied for one. Of the whole clearance area over

50 % of the residents favoured demolition. Thus, on aggregate, the council's demolition and rehousing policy *was* still meeting the wishes of a simple majority of the residents affected by it.

The bulk of the severe dissatisfaction with present housing was, however, concentrated in the one particular district, where over half of the residents reported major structural defects. And it was concentrated in certain types of household. For some, the case for or against demolition and moving to a council house was a fine one, involving a difficult balance of estimated profit and undoubted loss. For many, not far short of a majority, the balance lay in the opposite direction – the deficiencies in their present condition of life being greatly outweighed by the advantages, especially when weighed against the prospects of enforced migration. Some had made consider- able improvements on their own account, which they stood to lose. Inevitably *some* such houses must be expected in any demolition scheme, and their existence here and there or in small pockets can hardly be expected to hold back whole schemes. But these were *not* a few isolated cases. Many families had already invested in improvements – 54 % of Dennis's sample, and 74 % of those who were owner occupiers had done so. Most had acquired an internal water supply, and turned outhouses into bathrooms. The amenities absent were often ones whose loss was not felt simply because their addition was not seen as a benefit. The majority of those without an indoor toilet did not feel this to be a drawback. And why should they, providing there were 'adequate' facilities outside? Some even felt an indoor toilet was 'not nice', not hygienic, not polite.

Old dwellings cost less to live in than more modern ones. Housing consumes a higher proportion of income now than in 1900. Small wonder that there is a reluctance to move out of cheap accommodation, or that some people should prefer to have money spare for another purpose.

Cost apart, the attractions of council housing to many potential consumers are not overwhelming. Dennis reports that one third of Sunderland's housing list in the 1960s con- sisted of applications received within the previous year. Many of these were young married couples for whom an application to go on the list was only one of a number of options. Many of them took up other options or refused a house when it was offered. The smaller the family, the more likely that the house offered by the council would be refused,[6] with up to 81 refusals for every 100 houses let. Dennis comments, however, that 'while the housing list applicant can afford to express his preferences by waiting indefinitely, or even by choosing to forgo his application altogether, the slum-clearance family is deprived of its existing dwelling and is offered over a short period of time a limited number of alternatives'.[7] They had no way of knowing in advance that they would be offered a dwelling they would consider to be 'worth the money'. For not all council houses are equal. And in most cases a family moved to a council house would have, like it or not, to spend a higher proportion of their income on housing. It may be difficult for council officials to appreciate that a council tenancy may have fewer attractions in the eyes of potential residents than in their own. Many of those to be 'cleared' were owner/occupiers – 45 % of the households in the largest proposed slum-clearance area, and the number of owner/occupations was increasing. Owner/occupiers can keep improvement and maintenance at a level they decide themselves in the light of their own circumstances and preferences. They often enjoy greater freedom within their homes (e.g. to keep pets). Considerations which, when applied to people living in unpretentious Victorian housing, may seem minor to officials, but are real and worthy of respect.

Finally, the clearance family considers, money apart, the likely alternative housing. Does every prospect please? Flats and maisonettes are often disliked because of health, fire risk, lack of privacy, loss of space both internal and external, and the consequent need to abandon cherished but bulky items of furniture. High-rise flats have been the most suspect of all, tending to colour attitudes to council housing in general. This is not the only problem in housing allocation. If the council operates a 'tailor-made' system of housing allocation, the family to be housed gets a house to fit their present officially perceived needs, with nothing left over to spare. Thus a couple given a single-bedroomed house would be denied the extra space they might have been accustomed to use for putting up others of their family on occasional visits, or for storing goods they did not want to part with. In Sunderland in the 1960s this was so, even if they were prepared to *pay* for the extra space.

Then, people come to compare the life offered by new estates with that in the old, 'disordered', nineteenth-century districts they have to leave. Many of the planners' assessments of profit – open space, pedestrian pathways and so on, may seem comparatively minor gains to their users. Some of the 'amenities' indeed can be a positive menace, as focal points of vandalism, thuggery and worse. These can 'sour' the atmosphere of an estate, especially for the older residents. There is, too, the exchange of a tried and tested neighbourhood for an unknown quantity. In old, street-terraced neighbourhoods, many people appear to enjoy a balance of neighbourliness and privacy which suits their own preferences. It was the loss of the latter in the Sunderland clearances which most people feared and, on the council estates, experienced. Much post-war estate design was informed by a crude notion of working-class 'community' feelings as an end to be fostered, despite the well-attested yearnings of many people for privacy. Some of Sunderland's council estates[8] rated lower for privacy than the least private of the prospective clearance areas. Flats in particular offended on this score, since stairways and lifts meant that interaction with uncongenial neighbours was unavoidable. Quite a high proportion of those actually moved to new housing areas were 'unhappy' about their neighbours. Partly what people were missing was a neighbourhood in which they felt 'at home' because their life-style was confirmed by that of their neighbours.

The degree to which access to work and amenities, such as shops or a favourite pub or club, matters in a balance against other factors obviously varies from one household to another. In the poorest slum-clearance area in Sunderland 80 % were satisfied with access to work, twice the proportion satisfied at one of the peripheral council estates. Accessibility to social foci may be *the* big compensation for such ills as may attend living near the old heart of a town.

Me Dad can't walk . . . if you put him out to Town End Farm you might just as well shoot him up in a rocket and let him orbit in outer space.

Work? Just right! Shops? Couldn't get any better than this for anything like that! School? Just out of the back door! Church? Just down the street! Pubs and clubs? All round us! Town Centre? Only a threepenny bus ride![9]

Samples of bus journeys made necessary by transfer to council estates showed massive increases; in one group of families their total weekly journeys rose by 230%. The cost advantage of nearness to a place of work, measured in terms both of fares and of the capacity to eat meals at home, is often several pounds a week. Loss of easy access is loss, therefore, in financial, social and psychological terms. For some, the deprivation may be very severe.

This study concluded that 'in their own terms, large minorities, and in many cases, substantial majorities of families believe that on balance they would lose by being rehoused'.[10] But of course people may not always know what is in their own best interests. Objectively their conditions, however well loved, could have been baneful. Dennis shows, however, that not only was this not so for a substantial number, but also that, in any case, the officials made little serious effort to find out if it was or not. There were no written criteria for judgement. Visual inspection of externals was frequently carried out from a moving vehicle. Doorstep interviews on the subject of household amenities were typically completed in under two minutes. There was room for the suspicion that officials were not really interested in examining the housing, and that they had already made up their minds to condemn it.

Dennis's more recent study, *Public Participation and Planning Blight* brings the story into the post-Skeffington era of widespread rhapsodizing on the need for public participation in planning; this is particularly apt since one of the members of the Skeffington Committee was a senior official of the local authority in question. Evidently, in the author's view, nothing much had changed as far as the citizens were concerned. The development, over the years, of a more elaborate planning machinery appeared to enhance one particular by-product of planning – the output of uncertainties. One area had been scheduled, in the 1952 programme, for demolition in 1972. A revised programme in 1968 then envisaged 1991. Then the 1969 Housing Act, authorizing subsidies for houses which, after improvement, would have a further 'life' of 15 or 30 years, postponed the prospect indefinitely. The uncertainty thus blighted the area and its people's lives for two or more decades; but the cost to the officials was nil.

Nor would it seem that there had been much improvement either in the method of deciding which houses and streets merited 'treatment' or in the care taken to communicate such decisions to those affected. When one particular street was included in the clearance scheme the fact was not even reported in the local evening paper.[11] Then the revised plan for the street was not conveyed to the residents. The first they learned of it was when it was listed, along with 20 other areas for slum clearance in the official civic newspaper. 9 months before rehousing was due to begin, a resident was told it was 'anticipated' her house could be demolished 'within the next two years'. In the summer of 1973 the Housing Committee, without being given, or asking for, any evidence, approved the Medical Officer's recommendation that houses in this street be demolished as unfit for human habitation. The evidence arrived one month later. In fact the Committee Chairman agreed that half the houses were quite acceptable; but the majority went with the Medical Officer.

The grading of areas from worst to best continued to appear quixotic and at variance with common acquaintance of the district. However, the data had been processed by computer and was treated as correspondingly sacred. Some of the inspections, it later emerged, took place after the publication of the proposals.

Brave new Newcastle, perhaps

At Sunderland, as befits a smaller town, the planning was planning with a small 'p'. It was not greatly more than an ambitious scheme of slum clearance and rehousing, involving local public officials such as the housing department. In Newcastle upon Tyne the scene was altogether more elevated. One of the first cities to go overboard for planning as ideology, as the specialism of a profession, aimed at creating not merely renewal but a new world, this was Planning with a capital 'P'.

In 1958, Newcastle had 9 planners attached to the City Engineer's Department, dealing chiefly with development control. By 1966 there were 83 in an independent Planning Department.

The days of seedy elegance for this declining but humane city were over. The Labour party on the council, having acquired a leader of great and well-publicized vigour, had set out to do for the city what many of them had done for themselves, namely, to pull it up by the bootstraps. They touched nothing that they did not transform. Newcastle acquired, from the Ford Motor Company, a city manager. On the slopes where the terraced streets off the Scotswood Road had stood arose the Brazilia of the North (the phrase is not mine). At the other end of town municipal pomp and circumstance was given an appropriate setting in the Civic Centre, with its row of flambeaux, and carillon of bells playing 'The Blaydon Races' to encourage regional consciousness. At the same time, part of Grainger and Dobson's unique early Victorian townscape was torn down to make way for a luxury hotel (that was not in fact, built). No wonder the *Architect's Journal* named the leader of the council as its 'man of the year'.

With all this bustle afoot it was inevitable that the city's inner, older residential areas would come to be regarded as suitable cases for treatment. And in truth, something would have had to be done about them anyway. Rye Hill, for instance, an area just south-east of the city centre, was a classic 'twilight zone.' At one time an area of some distinction, it 'went down' earlier in this century, as people of means found suburbia more attractive. In recent years it has been the scene of what some have seen as a piece of urban idiocy notable even for a city that has seemed to specialize in it. Briefly, like Newcastle itself, Rye Hill's was a story of an area subjected to a glossy, ambitious but fundamentally ill worked out plan of redevelopment. While in the pipeline the plan caused a virtual paralysis of much of the area's natural life. Once initiated, too much professional and political 'face' was involved for it to be dropped. In his study of the episode, *The Evangelistic Bureaucrat*,[12] Jon Gower Davies charges that the people of Rye Hill were the helpless victims of a massive arrogance of power on the part of both politicians and professionals, allied seemingly to an invincible imperviousness to matters of fact or logic. At Rye Hill the surveys before the plan, alleges Davies, were designed to 'prove' the series of preconceptions espoused by the planners. The general paralysis induced by 'waiting for the comprehensive plan' itself helped to induce the very decline in upkeep alleged by the planners in the first place. For the piecemeal work of house maintenance, such as painting, repointing and so on, naturally came to a stop. The protracted delays were officially blamed on the insufficient powers contained in the planning acts. Eventually, following a change of political control on the city council, the plan was curbed; but only after the amount and quality of Rye Hill's housing had been reduced while its cost to residents had been raised.

Discussion

These studies show how 'planning' can easily become the name of a procedure by which bureaucratic/political power can range itself against the powerless even while aiming to do them good. It is not necessary to attribute anything but the best of intentions to those in powerful places in order to sustain this argument. The impersonal despotism of virtue, it has been said, is not the less despotic because it is virtuous.

There is no reason to believe that these studies could not have been replicated almost anywhere in Britain where town hall confronts the inner city. And, as in Newcastle, many of the same features are present when the battle lines are drawn up about something else – say the destruction of architectural heritage, or the carve up of townscape by motorway development. There is often the same 'adhockery' posing as science, the same 'pseudodata', the hurried mustering of arguments *after* the decision has been announced, the same sacrificing of the human to some professional or technological fashion.

Those who might be inclined to argue that a contest over say, offices versus homes in Southwark is of a different order of seriousness to one over the threatened demolition of say a Charles Rennie Mackintosh building in Glasgow are mistaken. The underlying threat is the same. Whenever something beautiful, ingenious, eccentric or historic is under attack, an aggression is being committed against the humane, just as much as when a street of homes is the victim. And, as like as not, as in Newcastle, the same configuration of people and attitudes will have been responsible.

These studies draw attention to the consequences of the merging of three forms of power, the political (in the party, policy-making sense), the bureaucratic, and what has been aptly termed[13] the 'datacratic'. On this evidence 'slum clearance' was conducted in a boorishly insensitive manner; when dressed up in all the finery of the planning ideology, the result appeared to be little different, since the pretensions of planning were grandiose out of all proportion to its modest capabilities. But neither case could be termed simply one of 'bureaucracy run wild', in the sense that the politicians had attempted, and failed, to stop some juggernaut organization from inexorably working its will. Far from it. The politicians were part of the system. Officials are not the only 'big' thinkers. So are politicians. Edward C. Banfield, in an appraisal of the Rye Hill study, argues that this was simply an example of British local government performing pretty much as it is supposed to.[14] If the scheme was misconceived, the error was made by the electorate which presumably put the Labour party in power in the city, in the hope/expectation that it would generate such schemes. Naturally, a change of council control to the Conservatives led to a change of course. Rye Hill was a success, not of planning to be sure, but of democracy. Whether or not we accept Banfield's argument, certainly the point holds that much criticism of 'planners' or other local government officials is wide of the mark in its omission of the political dimension. Politicians ought to be held responsible for the consequences of what they sanction.

What appears to have happened in both cases is that once the initial, political, decision to go ahead had been taken, the officials were left to get on with it, on the assumption that the working through of the programme was a technical, not a political matter. Hence, although it is the council, collectively, which is supposed to be the political master of the officials, and the councillor individually, who is supposed to be the medium of communication between people and government, Dennis avers that the 'planners' at Sunderland were quite out of councillor control. It was they, not the council members, who defended the proposals, using technical, planning grounds rather than referring to political decisions. And in private, their view of councillors was said to be that 'not only did the councillors know nothing; a more serious matter altogether, they were not entitled to know anything'.[15] They even went so far in this as to insist that letters be sent direct to them rather than to the Chairman of the Planning Committee.

Both critics would, however, insist that here were not cases of a true clash between expertise and democracy, since they would deny the presence of the former. The officials are accused of being unable to defend their plans against challenge; of insisting on the soundness of forecasts which turned out to be massively in error; and at the same time of also insisting on keeping all options open. Officials were highly reluctant to admit that their work was subject to all manner of uncertainties. They went on pumping out the current orthodoxy as if it was objective and unchangeable. That it was no such thing was proclaimed by the reversal in the 1969 Act, of the policy of comprehensive demolition.

This late change, of course, though welcome, was too late to save many of the people of the inner areas of the cities from the experiences described here. For them, it might be said that in the 1960s we had made a wilderness and called it redevelopment.

Chapter 3 What is Planning For?

> ... *a problem is identified by the ruling strata of society, a solution is devised and imposed on the population – subject, to be sure, to a limited veto of democratic elections which do not in practice make a great deal of difference to what is actually done. The march of science is relentless. The brief and unpleasant answer is probably that we need less science and more choice.*
> – David Eversley[1]

> *The goal-generalist evaluator makes a claim to rationality which, though it may be limited to a specific area of policy, is essentially a claim to wisdom.*
> – Alan A. Altschuler[2]

Town planning may be regarded as a necessary element in the management of a complex and changing urban society. It is more than anything else concerned with monitoring and coordinating changes in land use in and around the cities. But it is not just a matter of engineering and management. It also has been seen and used as part of the weaponry of social reform.

British town and country planning, however, had always been more than even these. It has a 'great tradition', with heroes and ideology to match. Since the late nineteenth century it has been one vehicle for the utopian strain in English liberal thought. And, as a movement, it has had, and continues to have, its successes.

The path of planning was easy, however, and its aims largely undisputed, while attention was focused on new developments on what were hitherto green fields. From the later 1950s on, however, planning as a specialized enterprise began to get under way inside the existing cities. The larger cities began to set up planning departments. And now the problems began. For it could well be argued that the great tradition had little to offer that had relevance to the problems of existing but decaying built-up areas. What planning had inherited from its founding fathers was a great and humane ambition quite out of scale with its actual equipment. There is nothing very surprising about this; it is characteristic of most sciences in their early stages.

One of the signs of the confusion into which 'planning' has been falling is the diffusion of the term. More and more people have been saying in effect 'we are all planners now'. After all, planning can be seen, as Altschuler puts it, as 'simply the effort to infuse activity with consistency and conscious purpose'.[3] As a result, some of the ills attributed to 'planning' may have relatively little to do with the activities of professional town planning as such. Architecture, for example, has also been floundering about in the search for urban form, and planners can hardly alone share the blame for the consequences of the more than somewhat totalitarian visions of Le Corbusier.

Again, a great deal of change is initiated by 'private' capital; by property developers for instance, which the planners (however defined) have been unable to stop and to which they must accommodate their plans as best they can. Centre Point was a failure of planning only in the sense that somebody should have had the power to stop it. And of course the ultimate sanction for planning activity rests with the politicians. Whether they are equipped to cope with this responsibility, or not, it is theirs.

The difficulty in resolving the question of what planning in the late twentieth-century city is for, is not made easier by the utterances of planners themselves. Planners are often rather cloudy about the desired end, or value to be maximized, in their work. Like many professions they tend to rather grand and somewhat empty generalizations when speaking of themselves. Inevitably, much of their day-to-day activity is concerned with technique and administration. But to what end? Generally we have to infer an ideology from a range of generalized statements and from specific actions, as contrasted with, say, a process whereby these flow naturally as the result of a clear

157

ends/means programme based on clearly evolved and widely agreed principles, as might be said to be the case of the medical and legal professions. It is the relative absence of the latter situation which makes it difficult to enter debate about the principles of planning and the means of effectuating them.

Let us, therefore, attempt to summarize some of the elements which critics have discerned as the ideology and purpose of planning. For, arguably, the most useful contribution the social scientist can make to planning is not so much as a supplier of factual information but as a tester of the assumptions underlying planning. These are of two types – assumptions about planning itself, and incorporated therein a range of rarely explicit assumptions about society. Five of these assumptions about planning are advanced by one commentator, Eric Reade.[4] One, planning is concerned with the best use of the limited supply of land. This is a view of appeal to the geographers who form an important component of the planning profession. It has an aura of being uncontroversial, 'scientific' and value-free. In fact, as it is about the allocation of resources, this view involves some of the biggest political questions of all. Secondly, it is about the built environment – an emphasis which rather ignores the human interaction that takes place therein or, at least, involves somewhat crude assumptions about the relationship between the two. This is stuff such as architectural dreams are made of, all too often. Thirdly, planning is a matter of engineering, a technical activity – building roads, towns, etc. to specifications that are objective and 'given', because already decided by someone else. For example, housing grown old or below standard must go – the end is agreed, only the question of means remains. But of course the ends are questionable. Fourthly, it is about teamwork – the coordination of various hitherto separately organized activities. Fifthly, it is about optimizing the performance of systems. Dennis comments caustically on planning as a 'coordinated framework of decisions', that in the Sunderland experience it has been close to being a 'synonym for confusion'. Dwellings in clearance areas were placed in a decision-making limbo. Families could not continue the normal processes of adaptation, not knowing when they might have to move, where they might have to move to, or what compensation they might get. Planning here, argue its critics, means the local authority keeps all its options open while preventing others from exercising theirs.

With his focus on planning in relation to slum clearance and rehousing, Dennis adds a political dimension to the evaluation of the planning ideology. There is the proposition that re-development is a public issue. It is not in the 'public interest' for me to retain a house which is structurally dangerous, en-courages disease, stunts my children, or prevents road improve-ments. Fine. But if my house is merely ugly, or spoils the town's image to visiting industrialists? Many demolitions, he suggests, have tended to be of houses offending in the latter ways, i.e., in highly vague other-regarding respects; they come in for treatment as if they were not private dwelling places at all, but expendable parts of a city's 'plant' to be renewed at will. Or again, replacing my house may be doing me a good turn. After all, my poverty or ill housing is not just my concern but everyone's. Ought not I then to be grateful? But, for charity I have no choice but to receive? And if I define the end product for me not as gain, but as hardship, who then is served?

The erasing of blots on the urban landscape has always been an important element in planning. The blots being defined arbitrarily. Thus, as Dennis concludes,

not only technical decisions but also moral judgements are properly in the hands of a skilled class of administrative officials and the destiny of slum clearance families is to be decisively moulded, not by their own fallible judgement but according to the intuitiveness of rare great minds and not according to their own scheme of morality but according to the edicts of an enlightened profession.[5]

The above criticisms indicate the range of activities and pre-tensions which cluster together under the umbrella of town planning. It is a confusing mixture. Planning is about virtually everything. But there is one thing more, it is about the future.

The proposition that the idea of progress is dead is one of

the oddest of myths. It is alive and well and living in the Town Hall, wherever two or three of the more visionary city politicians and planners are gathered together. The best way to stop the march of progress would appear to be to have something valuable to preserve against it. If what you have to preserve is, say, the Vale of Aylesbury – beautiful, affluent and southern, there is probably a chance. If none of these, the outlook is unpromising. So brace yourself for a spot of future shock.

There is a notion, popularized by Alvin Toffler, that somehow 'the future' is here already. The problem is how people are to adapt to 'the roaring current of change . . . the process by which the future invades our lives'.[6] Toffler calls attention to the shattering stress and disorientation that we induce in individuals by subjecting them to too much change in too short a time. This is 'future shock'. But the shock is man-induced. The acceleration of change is not, *pace* Toffler, an elemental force, to which we must adapt. Resistance to it is not irrational. As change is man-made, so its pace and direction must be man-controlled.

The utopian inheritance of planning, the undoubted idealism of planners, and the obvious fact that we *must* plan to account for our future needs, makes planning an activity liable to the charge of artificially inducing 'future shock', of adapting man to his future and not vice versa. In recent years, for example, we have had the post-Buchanan mania for 'adapting the city to the car' involving among other things the construction of expensive and intrusive urban motorways. We have had Stansted–Cublington–Foulness, and in the Rye Hills of the cities, extremes of 'modernization' of housing which amounted in practice to jam today, at tomorrow's prices.

It is manifestly easy for the central vision in planning to be captured by one fashion after another. High-rise flats. No high-rise flats. Urban motorways. No urban motorways. Low densities. High densities. Low densities again. 'Community' and so on. Planning is not, of course, alone in this. Ideologies which are strong on the benefits of some technology or other, but crude on its application are quite common amongst new professions (which in turn are often staffed by 'new men'). The techniques help in the process of professionalization. They help to give the activity legitimacy, especially in the eyes of its own practitioners. But when something goes manifestly wrong, they leave their adherents naked and directionless. And so the next fashion comes in.

The point was put by a leading American planner, Melvin Webber, who told the Town Planning Institute in 1968 that 'planning is acquiring that status that the priestly arts once enjoyed'.[7] In whose eyes? And where are the priests of yesteryear? Gone, and their mysteries with them.

One is never quite sure, however, whether the critics of planning have not overdone their task and are frequently shying at Aunt Sallies of their own erection. Often the planners' faults have been to appear to claim too much for their craft. Or to claim too much certitude as the basis of their arguments. But we have to plan on the best evidence available at the time, and this can be notoriously misleading. For example, at the most basic level, estimated population, we have the famous case of Britain's disappearing population growth. The United Kingdom's estimated population by 2001 was put at 74 million in 1965. By mid 1971, 11 million had been clipped off this figure. Add to this the difficulty of estimating future patterns of internal migration, future prospects for the availability and cost of land, both inside existing cities and elsewhere, the changing pattern of availability and cost of fuel, the impossibility of accounting for future shifts in political direction, and many other greater and lesser variables, and we at once realize we are planning in a state of extreme uncertainty. Yet plan we must. Planners (and politicians) would only be at fault if they were to hand down as matters of sure and certain prediction information which they knew, or ought, claiming a competence, to know, was at best provisional. It may be true that, as Davies has put it, 'in many of the subjects (and they are legion) on which planners pronounce there is simply no such thing as an objective body of knowledge allied to a coherent theory which can be used as a basis for rational decision-making'.[8] Nobody should be pilloried, however, for trying to act on the basis of knowledge that seems valid at the time, even if it is proved false later, provided it is used with due respect to its scope and limits. All knowledge is imperfect. In those who use knowledge about society to change society, there is much in the arrogance or humility with which the knowledge is handled.

Much of the difficulty lies within the field of communication. Attacks on experts' use of specialist language may come, at times, close to a modern form of Luddism, but, like Luddism, they can represent, nevertheless, genuine frustration. For scientific language *can* be used to mystify; it is easy to use it to dress up, in dazzling clothes, a decision arrived at for the most arbitrary and unscientific of reasons.

Criticism of the pretensions of planning and probing of the purposes of planning in society are inextricable from each other. In particular, critics are concerned to stress the social, as contrasted with physical, dimension of planning. In his *Town Planning in its Social Context*, G. E. Cherry urges that 'the fate of social planning for too long has been to be regarded as an afterthought rather than a prior consideration',[9] owing to the hegemony of the physical planning disciplines within planning. Planners ought not to hold a lofty view (at any rate as planners) as to the purposes of society. They ought to concern themselves with more specific objectives, namely the promotion of human contact, the consideration of minority group interests, the strengthening of the social services, the ordering of priorities in decision-making. In short, social planning strategy as Cherry sees it should be designed to limit the social, physical and economic constraints that operate in the environment. The planners' role should be 'permissive as much as authoritarian'.

Cherry's formulation possibly does not go far enough. To David Eversley, social planning is an entirely different activity from traditional physical planning. It is concerned not only with the housing stock and environmental quality but also with the whole range of social services, the employment structure, and with the problems of the disadvantaged groups in society. It involves 'the total effort by all agencies to achieve changes in the physical environment, and in the economic and social structure which exists within that environment, in the pursuit of improvements in the living standards of an urban population'.[10] It is, in effect, part of the new corporate management. It is openly and explicitly political, in that it is concerned with the distribution of goods, services and economic prospects between different sections of society. Or, as Cullingworth has put it 'Planning is not a technical means to a political end: it is itself part of the political process.'[11]

Planning thus should be *goal-explicit* and *user-oriented*, in the terms of Herbert Gans.[12] There must be, Gans argues, first, a clear set of goals or objectives, and second, clearly formulated criteria by which to decide on priorities within these, since resources are limited. Only with these ends clearly established, urges Gans, can we proceed thirdly to the elaboration of means – the plans and projects themselves. Hitherto in Britain and America planning systems have been weak on the first two, crucial stages, with the result that massive effort has gone into activites whose objectives were poorly worked out, or rested on assumptions never made explicit. It is because of this, he would argue, that planning has usurped the boundaries of its competence, since the critical problem in the above formulation is 'whose goals, whose priorities?'

Certainly not those of the planners. I may need a taxi badly, but this does not give the taxi-driver any greater right to decide on my destination. He has his sphere of competence, but he operates within my directive. Gans points out, that planning has been typically the approach of the middle-class reformer; with the master-plan, the paper plan for a total community, every function prescribed, as his typical obsession, from the days of Titus Salt, through the garden cities movement, to the new towns of our own era. Few of the master-planners, Gans suggests, have ever paused to consider whether they had a right to regulate say, leisure behaviour, or the location and type of housing. This may have been true of planning as a profession, but it was certainly not true of English planning in its origins. Titus Salt, W. H. Lever and the others made no bones about what they were doing. In their benevolently autocratic way they were conscious of a right to determine how people should live. Here was no myth of value-free planning.

There is indeed no value-free planning; what we have to ensure is that the values and goals it serves are determined not by the planners but in the public market-place of politics. Here clearly, a major (and exacting) part of the planners' role in a situation where others, non-planners, make the key decisions, will be, in Senior's words 'to catalyse the manifestation of his community's political and social values, in time enable them to shape planning policies, by postulating alternative solutions and explaining their value implications'.[13]

In an open, goal-explicit system, as Gans is keen to emphasize, there is a potentially vital role for the planner in political debate on planning – as a citizen and professional man rather than as a public servant. For having seen the goals and values that are being served, he has as much right as any citizen and indeed, perhaps even, as an especially informed one, a duty, to act in any politically legitimate way to point out to the decision-makers 'what implicit goals they are pursuing and with what consequences'.[14] This, of course, would run clean counter to the British tradition whereby public servants do not engage in public debate. It is a tradition which, in many fields, we might do well to modify.

If planning is to be 'social' and 'user-oriented', a central concern must be how to give effect to the user's definition of the situation. This is not easy, as is demonstrated elsewhere. On the citizens' side, 'participation' is full of problems. On the planners' side, it is acknowledged by David Eversley, former Chief Strategic Planner for the GLC, in his important book *The Planner in Society*,[15] that much of the blame for the friction between planner and planned is the planners' own fault. He endorses the criticism of planners' increasing reliance on 'scientific' methods and unintelligible language. Planners have been associated, rightly or wrongly, with huge, intrusive and perhaps comparatively useless developments (roads, offices). They have been made scapegoats by discontented idealists and by the media; and many of these critics, he replies scathingly, are unrepresentative, self-appointed people who have no appreciation of the complexity of society. But, he argues, the planning profession has not responded well to this mood. It has been defensive, not troubling to understand the complaints, resenting its own young Turks who have got involved in community action. Moreover, he writes elsewhere, in the midst of a frantic search for still greater refinement and precision in planning methods, 'a drastic deterioration of urban life' in ways people care about, has not been averted. Almost every one of the most popular policies in planning 'has enormous drawbacks both for the intended recipient of the improvement advocated or for others'.[16]

What, therefore, is needed? Let us simply, at this stage, conclude with some general, but vital, principles:

1. '. . . it is essential that those whose values are being affected should find maximum scope for the expression of their preferences and that these preferences should be seriously considered as data: the wish to be rehoused by the council, the wish to be modernised, the wish to be left alone.'[17]

2. Means of communication between the consumers and the providers should be a chief study for all, including planners, involved in urban politics. Proposals for change in a neighbourhood must pass the preliminary test of communicability in terms understood by those affected.

3. Planning education should incorporate the principle that understanding the world of those affected by planning, and the consequences of public policy for them, is at least as important as training in the theory and technology of planning.

4. Encouragement should be given to any form of neighbourhood action or voice which seems viable, provided it can establish its claim as a bona fide expression of local interests.

5. Procedures involving people in involuntary changes in their

lives, whether for their own good or that of the wider community, must be such that as far as possible *they* can see the process as fair and the results, for them, as benign. 'Government is a question of compromise, of compensation for those injured in the process of change.'[18] For surely, as Rawls has put it, 'the fundamental criterion for judging any procedure is the justice of its likely results'.[19]

A note on authority

Many of the difficulties which we have got into over bureaucratic power, political control and popular participation have a basis in underlying uncertainties, some would even say in a crisis, concerning the nature of authority in society. By what criteria are we to judge whether we should accept as legitimate the claims of a person or group of people to make decisions affecting our lives? The highest political debate, of course, has always been about this. But the form that it takes is constantly changing and arguably the advent of big government demands that we approach it anew.

Robert Dahl, in *After the Revolution?*[20] suggests that there are three main criteria for judging whether a process for making binding political decisions is valid and rightful. The first, and perhaps most obvious, is that of *personal choice*. The problem here is to reconcile personal choice with our nature as social beings; hence the need for some modification of individual freedoms, for mutual guarantees to restrain majorities and protect minorities, and so on. This much, one might venture, is tacitly understood by most people as a central element in democratic life. Dahl's other criteria may be less well understood. The second is that of *competence*. We accept it when we acknowledge that someone has a right to make decisions affecting us, his right resting on the qualification of superior knowledge or skill. Parents claim this *vis-à-vis* children – in varying degrees no doubt, but they all claim it. Again, I have no desire to travel in a plane where superior competence on the part of the pilot is not the sole criterion for all important in-flight decisions. These are, however, extremely clear-cut cases. For one thing, the pilot's competence is, hopefully, beyond reasonable dispute (at any rate by the passengers) and it has a very clear-cut boundary. The pilot knows, for example, that the reason for my journey is none of his business. For another, there is no room for dispute between the claims of competence and personal choice here. There is a clear point where personal choice ends (when I join the plane) and competence takes over. Many other cases are less clear cut, however. We may not agree that, say, an official or professional man's claim to competence *is* soundly based; we may dispute where lies the boundary between action based on competence or expertise, and action based on fashionable notions. And we may decide for ourselves that the proper mix of competence and personal choice impels us to forgo some of the competence. Most peoples prefer self-determination to government, however more efficient, by others. Again, as Sennett points out, a 'disordered' environment is to be preferred, often, in human terms, to an ordered one. As Dahl says, no system of decision-making will perfectly meet both criteria. Most likely, we will try to find some optimum mix that meets neither fully.

The same holds true when we add the third criterion, that of *economy*. Methods of decision-making vary in their capacity *vis-à-vis* the scarce and valuable resources of time and effort. A process must be seen to be reasonably efficient in its use of our time and effort. If some activity proves to be heavily demanding, then we generally require its product to be commensurately worthwhile, from some viewpoint or other, whether it be social rewards, personal satisfaction or getting something done. And in assessing worthwhileness, we have to bear in mind that there is no bank of time. Time spent is time irrecoverable for some other purpose. Government by mass meeting, for most people, offends against this criterion. Hence it gives, usually, great power into the hands of those activists for whom the political ends *do* justify this time consuming means.

There is no need to labour the point of the relevance of these considerations to the political processes of cities. But they are considerations, not rules. In themselves they are politically neutral. In each particular action, it is for each interested party to judge in his own case the profit and the loss as between the criteria; and, importantly, to judge the claims of others to wield authority on the grounds of these criteria. Different men will judge by different values. The ideal mix of the three, for any association of people, will depend upon their own definition of desired ends and desired means. Certain generally applicable conclusions do stand out, however. If a group of actors are claiming, in effect, power over others on the basis of competence, this claim must be open to scrutiny. There is a difference between technical knowledge and fashionable notions. People involved in planning activities, for example, must be prevented from presenting the latter in the guise of the former. People should have the right to reject expertise, or the most economical procedures, if they feel these a threat to personal choice. If personal choice *must* be curbed, the reasons, in terms of other people's choices, or in terms of the costs incurred according to the other criteria, must be shown openly.

Decision-makers and methods of decision-making do not have authority as of right. It is conferred upon them. Authority in a democratic society can only be acceptable if its claims are visible and can stand up to scrutiny via open processes.

Part Five   **Citizens: the Emergent Dimension**

Chapter 1 Participation and Community Action – for What?

> *There is some failure of orthodox politics. They fail to deal satisfactorily with the matters which face a modern community. They fail also to give people satisfaction or to make them feel that their wishes are adequately expressed.*
> – Jo Grimond[1]

> *Though it does contribute to human dignity and is not something to be despised, sharing in decisions is no panacea, no general cure for the evils of injustice and arbitrary power.*
> – Barrington Moore[2]

Cries for increased citizen participation in decision-making have been coming thick and fast in recent years. We have heard them in relation to town planning, to industry, and to a host of other points at which the apparent powerlessness of the many is held up in contrast with power arbitrary, anonymous, bureaucratic. Yet, 'under the banner of participation march a motley crowd, with a variety of objectives and programmes'.[3] An extremely wide spectrum of activity tends to be treated together under this heading. Let us confine our attention to that dimension of the participation/community action syndrome which is aimed at influencing the policy-making/administrative process and expanding the existing concept of democracy at the local level to allow a larger role for the citizen in the making of decisions. (Some, of course aim far beyond this.) Here, we have had much more argument about possible tactics than about the reasons why more participation and community action are needed in the first place. These are often assumed to be self-evident.

Arguments for increased participation are often extremely woolly in conception and lacking in firm grounding in evidence about how people actually behave. If we are to make any headway we must be clear both about the purposes of what is being advocated and about its prospects of becoming reality.

Participation then, by whom, for what and why? Justifications for increased participation are often presented as part of a package in which not one, but several different benefits are held out. The contents of the mixture may vary from advocate to advocate, but the three main ingredients are, health of democracy, self-fulfilment of citizens, getting something done. It is a mixture which, in one form or another has echoes both in the populistic leftist writings of recent years on both sides of the Atlantic, and in the central tradition of liberal democratic theory going back as far as J. S. Mill.

A recent exponent of this tradition, Dennis F. Thompson,[4] emphasizes the first two ingredients, listing among the ends served by citizen participation, checks on 'sinister interests', by which it is implied not well-meant error, but the abuse of power; a sense of wholeness of being which citizens may obtain from involvement in public affairs; political stability arising from this satisfaction; the expression of as many viewpoints as possible, since only those affected by a policy can really say *how* it affects them; finally, he points out, action increases consciousness and hence involvement is an essential part of the process whereby people gain that awareness of their interests which they must have before they can promote them.

A powerful element in this thinking is that which associates democracy with self-realization or a sense of personal effectiveness on the part of the citizens, and hence argues for increased 'participation' as a means of enhancing both. Another notable proponent of this view has been Carole Pateman in her *Participation and Democratic Theory*.[5] Much of her argument stems from the well-known correlation found by Almond and Verba in their *The Civic Culture*[6] between levels of participation in decision-making and feelings of 'political efficacy'.

The third ingredient concerns needs, power and action. Power is, after all, among other things, the capacity to get things done, and those with the greatest needs generally tend to be somewhere near the bottom of the participation heap. Participation here is justified on instrumental grounds. It is about attempting to redraw the rules of the power game to the advantage of those who have hitherto been the losers (e.g. in terms of housing, employment, income, etc.). This, rather than the other two, is what radical community action advocates have in mind. Dahl links this with the 'health of democracy' argument when he remarks that 'until and unless we reach greater parity in the distribution of political resources, other steps towards democratisation are like treating tuberculosis with aspirin, or air-dropping marshmallows to famine victims'.[7]

The three elements, when combined, can add up to a pretty heady mixture. One such, for example, is provided by Jon Rowland in his book *Community Decay*.[8] For him, participation and community recovery are to be seen in world-historical terms, as a means towards 'self-actualization', the overcoming of alienation, etc. This book begins with the Darwinian implications of the Apollo missions, proceeds with a tour around the Protestant ethic and the condition of man under industrial capitalism, and, via a useful study of an area of north London, concludes with the gospel of neighbourhood power. The 'community folk moot' will be largely autonomous. It 'will take decisions affecting its own education, leisure, housing and communications facilities', and will even deal with its own sanitation, though inexplicably, the 'higher' authority will provide the drains. As a result, 'the original concept of community will return'[9], self-realization may be realized, and conditions will improve. 'The prospect of participation with the potential contribution of everyone means a stop to the feelings of powerlessness and apathy, and a move towards a positive mobility orientation.'[10] Towards a what?

God protect a good idea from its friends. It is a bit much for one idea to have to bear the burden of responsibility for largely rescuing us from the human condition.

It is clear that, in some forms, the mixture of justifications for participation is open to fairly serious objection. So too are each of the individual elements, 'health of democracy', 'health' of the citizen, and the instrumental argument. In assessing any justification for or experiment in participation we ought to require of it that there be a clear conception of what it is meant to achieve, how it relates to the rest of the mechanism for making decisions, and that it bear some relation to existing evidence as to how people actually behave.[11] The latter is perhaps the weakest feature of the whole syndrome, but it is not the only one. We shall come to it later.

Professor Thompson's strongest suit is his argument on democratic grounds. However, it might be easily demonstrated that the pressure groups which have long been part of liberal democratic politics can perform some of the functions, such as the expression of interests, more effectively than 'citizen participation'. The 'abuse of power' may, *prima facie*, be checked by minority involvement just as effectively as by mass involvement, provided that the minority have an effective means of so doing. And to foster one of his democratic values may well be at the expense of another. 'Developing consciousness' is likely to be a process involving a quite different 'frequency' or time scale, as effectively combating some specific abuse of power. Then 'participation' may be good for the body politic, but how much of it is? Too much, and we have a recipe for immobilism, with decision-making rendered almost impossible.

Similar objections may be raised when the 'health of the citizen' argument is added in. 'Participation' may be good for people – but so is gardening, football and a host of other things. Besides, this argument undervalues the extent of opportunities for participation already available. If people do not take up the opportunities which exist for participation in the life of political parties, trade unions and voluntary organizations, what reason is there to believe that some new form of participation in local decision-making would be different in its appeal? If people do not choose to define personal self-fulfilment in this way, they can hardly be made to. In fact, of course, many millions of people do participate, by proxy, through the activities of the myriad voluntary and professional pressure-groups which have emerged. Few major decisions in Britain take place without the involvement directly or by proxy of millions of citizens as members of political parties, pressure groups, trade unions and professional organizations, business and industrial organizations, religious bodies, residents of regions and cities, and so on. Doubtless new opportunities for active participation *would* appeal to some people – probably those active already, for the most part, but the evidence that they would be a means of self-fulfilment to vast new armies of formerly inactive, apathetic citizens is rather lacking.

Mrs Pateman's argument is basically derived from the research finding that people who have, or believe they have, skill at manipulating their immediate environment, are more likely to be active in politics, or at least to feel that any potential action on their part is likely to be of political value. Conversely, those who have a low sense of personal power are less likely to participate in politics. If, therefore, popular participation is only an exercise in which people acquire those manipulative skills, it might still be a valuable one, provided the circle could be broken. The difficulty with this is that correlations are explicanda, not explanations. Mrs Pateman has to concede that after all it remains an open question whether the participatory ideal is realistically based upon evidence as to human behaviour.

Professor Thompson argues that the evidence of social science is not as incompatible with the arguments for 'citizen democracy' as might at first be imagined, and that, in any case, evidence about present behaviour is particularly inconclusive when applied to proposals for radical change, since the latter would alter the 'constants' on which empirical generalizations are based. As things stand now, however, there is a substantial weight of empirical evidence that participation at any other than the most simple levels is not very great. Below the level of a general election, voting turn-out is a minority activity, the more so as one considers the inner wards of cities. In inner Liverpool wards, local election turn-out is generally 20–30 %. Nor is there much evidence of a demand for 'participation' as such. The evidence points instead to the growth of a more purely instrumental or consumerist attitude to politics, in which people want not so much governments which will enable them to participate themselves, but which will 'deliver the goods'. Antony Barker comments, 'the politicians have ample grounds for sticking to their job of providing public services such as housing and schools and taking broad responsibility for their achievements at election time and through opinion poll findings'.[12]

While working-class people are as capable of organizing things as anyone else, as witness friendly societies, trades unions, sporting associations and political parties, they appear reluctant to join in some forms of activity to which middle-class people seem attracted. The amenity society, parent–teacher association, civic society or residents' association is a type of association which often relies less on numbers than on the quality of membership and the kinds of influence they can bring to bear. The orientation of members is often expressive rather than directly instrumental, and there is often the element of participation for social rewards. Goldthorpe *et al.* found at Luton[13] that residents of the new working-class estates were home-centred. They belonged to typically working-class associations such as angling or allotments' societies – to the extent of 1·5 of these per man. Their social life centred on the pub and the working men's club. They were not interested in joining voluntary associations, dominated by people with verbal skills, from different social backgrounds – often in fact the sort of people with whom they found themselves in conflict at work. The clash of norms which such mixing involves, may create stresses avoidable easily through withdrawal or not joining at all. The same of course may be said in the reverse direction, of middle-class people who get involved in predominantly working-class organizations.

It is not hard to point to instances where a voluntary association has flourished during the early 'pioneering' days of a housing estate. The new situation creates common adversity. Similarly in older areas of cities under the impact of, say, planning proposals. But most of these have not lasted long in the stage of their initial enthusiasm and before long have died or regressed to the level of yet another amenity association run by, and perhaps for, a small group who simply like doing that sort of thing. For example, in Camden, meetings held to discuss the Greater London Development Plan attracted about 0·1 % of the population, and of this about half the people were councillors, officers and representatives of civic and other societies. On the other hand, people in a neighbourhood area do turn out to meetings and form active, if short-lived, associations, when a council road proposal is made affecting the neighbourhood. The public are aroused by threats to their way of life rather than opportunities to participate. The evidence tends to indicate that most cases of 'participation' in planning are motivated by immediate self-interest and usually have a conservative, i.e. change-resisting tenor.

Pahl[14] suggests four reasons why such local activity rarely lasts long:

1. It is not difficult to get people involved in a campaign to secure amenities, but much more problematic to administer them once they *are* secured. Difficulty may arise from factional disputes and lack of authoritative leadership.

2. Residents' action has to compete for the citizens' attention with other concerns, activities and organizations, social, political, religious, etc.

3. Deprivation itself inhibits the social action of the deprived. (It was Cobbett who remarked that you cannot agitate a man on an empty stomach. In other words, those in most need are often precisely those rendered least capable of taking collective action about it.)

4. Adjustment to problems tends to be individualistic, especially in situations of high housing mobility, such as in 'twilight' areas or amongst incomers to new estates. Unless there is a sense of common objectives, there will hardly be a common desire for collective action.

It is a formidable list. In short, it is starry-eyed to assume that in most cases there is a reservoir of popular enthusiasm waiting to be tapped. In Britain, to date, official city government may not have made much of an effort to tap it. But there are familiar reports from around the world that 'considerable effort is required to induce people to serve on committees, to form opinions on local issues, and to hold their elected representatives responsible for the conditions of urban life'.[15]

Certain types of political activists, consumed with their own passion for action, tend to assume that there is some removable blockage in 'consciousness' which prevents people from seeing things as they ought. Few misreadings of human nature have caused more misery. In the case of the present question it is not such a harmful delusion, perhaps, but it is certainly well to be rid of it.

In the third, the instrumental or 'getting things done' argument, the case for expanding the scope of local political processes is couched more usually in terms of 'community action' (or some such phrase) rather than 'participation'. Within the framework of this discussion it is reasonable and convenient, to include the two together. Here, the argument is that if citizens, particularly (though not exclusively) organized on a neighbourhood level, can gain some power in the making of the decisions that affect them, then it is hoped that some generally desired social goals will be brought nearer – a more urgent attack on housing conditions, perhaps, or better social services for a neighbourhood, more sensitive housing and planning procedures, greater sensitivity to consumer preferences, and so on. The range of people who march behind the participation banner for reasons to do with the needs/power syndrome is vast. For the more politically minded, 'participation' may well be a dirty word when contrasted with 'action'. The latter may imply activity which explicitly challenges the norms and the values of the dominant political system (such, for example, as squatting). At this end of the spectrum, action centring on a specific goal is likely to be seen by activists to have also a general consciousness-raising dimension to it.

At this point, therefore, the question not simply of the ends, or justification, of participation, but the means whereby it is pursued, becomes critical. In their study of the position of the urban poor in the urban power structure, *Power and Poverty*, Bachrach and Baratz[16] discern two main modes of participation. Firstly, participation as a form of grass-roots activity undertaken by citizens on their own initiative. Implicit in this view is a belief in 'participation' as a chief means whereby the poverty-stricken can acquire the power and influence needed to enhance their economic and social life-chances. This conception Bachrach and Baratz label *interest-oriented participation*. In the second formulation, participation is seen as involving a collaborative relationship between those who give help and their 'clients' or beneficiaries. Here the implication is that the poor do not take action on their own account but by joining in the making of decisions about the type of services they receive will be enabled not only to get the particular kind of help they judge appropriate to their needs, but in the process will be helped to overcome feelings of alienation and 'acquire a sense of individual worth'. This is termed *cooptative participation*.

Interest-oriented participation is, of course, something which in theory our pluralistic politics already allows for. It is merely a question of getting in on the game. All that any group of citizens needs is the resources with which to play. And the necessary resources for any political game are just what the poor in the inner cities have not got – organization, expertise and cash. For a start, the political consciousness or sense of collective self-interest of the poor is generally rather weak, as is their sense of civic competence. Understandably they lack confidence in the efficacy of political activity as a means of achieving anything. The question is therefore, how interest-oriented participation, grass-roots action, can be got off the ground. In practice, much of the work will be done by an élite corps of 'community action specialists', perhaps outsiders to the area in question. However it is engendered, can this really be a means of the urban poor 'taking off' into acquiring a consciousness of collective self-interest, and growing in preparedness to act upon it in a struggle for a greater share of

179

the available resources? It is, considering everything, a pretty tall order.

Cooptative participation, whereby the energies and interests of the poor and powerless are not bent so much towards the acquisition of a measure of autonomous political power as channelled towards the goals which higher political authorities have already established, is the form of participation more likely, in practice, to emerge. This may amount to little more than an attempt by officials, who genuinely consider themselves to be acting in the 'best interests' of those whose future they are dealing with, to explain their proposals and to accept such marginal suggestions for change as may be compatible with their overall plan strategy. This is often despised, but perhaps it ought not to be. In many cases it would be in itself a gain, and one that could be built on. Moreover the kind of marginal suggestions emerging may be of a kind which mean little to the overall plan, but much to the citizens making them.

Generally, however, cooptative participation entails the acceptance by the participators of overall goals established elsewhere, and cooption can therefore be a new means of serving the interest of those with the power. In North Kensington, for example, cooperation between the council and the various radical groups is, says John Dearlove, 'a technique to control disturbance and channel dissent'.[17] A collaborative relationship between a radical group and the council is one where the former becomes a junior partner whose activities are channelled into the preordained goals of the authorities. The spontaneous and disruptive potentialities of their activities are thus offset. Hence defenders of the status quo, if subtle, are just as likely to find cooptative participation by citizens a valuable device as those who are out to create changes. The result of cooptative participation may be that demands for reallocations of resources are prevented from reaching the decision making stages. This can be a subtle way of facilitating what Bachrach and Baratz have called the making 'non-decisions'. That is to say, a means by which demands for change in the existing allocation of benefits and privileges in the community can be suffocated before they are even voiced; or kept covert; or killed before they gain access to the relevant decision-making arena; or failing all these things, maimed or destroyed in the decision implementing stage of the policy process.[18]

Any advocate of participation who holds out a prospect of benefits to a neighbourhood must make clear how the chosen means contribute to the attainment of these ends. For if emphasis is placed on the material results of action or participation, rather than on participation itself, it is an open question whether participation really can attain them, whether they cannot be more effectively gained by other means, and indeed whether it might not be the case that 'participation' is a positive hindrance to their attainment. Popular participation in decision-making and efficient decision-making may not always be inimical to each other, but common sense suggests that often they will be. As Geraint Parry points out, 'efficiency' is a problem in itself and impossible to compute, but a cumbersome process could well leave individual participants worse off *vis-à-vis* other values. 'If greater planning blight is the consequence of greater participation in planning then some individuals may find that the costs of participation are high indeed.'[19]

The final consideration is, who participates? The greatest danger with the undiscriminating advocacy of 'power to the people' is that it might result in a weakening of governmental capacity to achieve many of the objectives the advocates themselves want attained, while placing power in the hands, not of 'the people', but of a chaos of small groups of committed activists. And then we are back at square one. 'People's democracy' in any of its multivariate guises, has nothing to do with democracy and no more to do with 'the people' than the visions of any other clique of self-appointed prophets. It is no answer to the problem of making government responsive, to make it vulnerable to the pressure of those who merely shout the loudest, proclaiming their own highly particular version of the future.

The greatest charge against the participationist case is

probably that of simple irrelevance. In itself, it cannot build the homes, end the poverty, or whatever. Politically, 'participation' and 'community action' activities, taken in their widest sense, are vulnerable to the opposite dangers of cooptation on the one hand and impotent independence on the other. The flurry of 'community action' in recent years has had, at best, mixed results in terms of influence on Town Hall attitudes and policies. There has been much emphasis in discussion on tactics, on perceptions of the gains or losses at stake in 'community action' efforts, but much less on the perceptions of activism held by the central policy-makers themselves. What becomes of activism if those with the power to do things the activists want, react negatively to them and their message? Dearlove's study suggests that in the important case of Kensington this has been largely the case.

The very success of the Liberal Party's 'community politics' activities in the early 1970s underlines the point. 'Community politics' tends to concentrate on what often seems peripheral or even trivial, in its attempts to evoke citizen involvement. If the power structure appears unassailable on any of the more central fronts, it is natural to turn in frustration to where there *is* an opening – in the politics of the broken pavement. At best one can say of 'community politics' that it evokes a cry of pain against bureaucratic insensibility. It appears almost frivolous, however, set beside the problems of urban housing and urban poverty; and as a contribution to the question of 'participation' it is not very impressive either, since it has neither an evident relationship to policy-making, nor indeed any clear new concept of what citizenship entails.

It might appear, from what has been said, that 'participation' is a concept so weak in justification and so beset with difficulties of realization that citizens had better waste no further time pursuing it. Yet it would be a mistaken conclusion. This has been a plea not against participation but for clarity.

The case for encouraging the breathing of new life into local democracy remains a strong one, however strange and disappointing *some* of the resultant forms of that life might be. For the contrary case for the continuance unchanged of the present method of conducting the affairs of our cities is not appealing. It can be strongly argued that the existing representative system on its own is not an adequate check on the potential abuse of power, especially in the fields of planning and the administration of welfare services. It is *always* a good time to be exploring new means of making power responsive. It cannot but be a good thing to have the urban political system opened up to the invigorating breezes of criticism and fresh ideas, from whatever quarter they may blow. If some of these seem invalid, or premature, there is a market-place of ideas which will dispose of them. The same is true of experiments in participation and community action. And no doubt these will not build the houses, end the poverty, or whatever, but the effort may have justification elsewhere, in providing a challenge to national and local policy-makers and a bid for public opinion in a world where those who cannot make their voices heard or their muscles felt are very liable to neglect. The vast increase in the scope of governmental activity, national and local, makes all citizens clients of government more than ever before. Those who have to wear the shoe should not be denied any opportunity to say where it pinches; should have effective means of obtaining from government, and keeping it to, in Professor Thompson's words a 'declaration of intention to treat individuals' claims about their own interest with respect'.[20]

There is much that is sterile about the debate on participation. The mere good feelings on the one hand, the mere cries of pain on the other. Despite this, it *is* about something important. What we have done here is to list ingredients. Whether or not they can be made to add up to a digestible product depends upon getting the quantities right and doing the mixing carefully; and on this there is room for disagreement between those of different political tastes.

Chapter 2 Public Involvement in Planning

I am for democracy in all spheres of life, cultural, economic and social as well as political, for I do not believe anyone has the definitive conception of the purpose of life.

– Herbert J. Gans[1]

Citizen participation is not a means of achieving consensus. On the contrary it is a means of establishing conflicting views.

– J. B. Cullingworth[2]

The idea of giving weight in planning to the public dimension has become so enthroned in recent years that a genuflexion in its direction would appear, for most writers or speakers on planning, to have become almost obligatory. Yet the word (if one may be forgiven the metaphor) is still not made flesh.

Here, we start from the assumption that it would be 'a good thing' if it were, and take a look at current efforts, with their implications and difficulties, to make public involvement in planning more of a reality.

At first sight, the evidence before us is discouraging. A vast range of planning decisions, major and minor, have met with little public debate and only the token involvement of non-specialists. The most notable cases of public arousal have been cases of reaction, belated, by people with a status quo to defend.

Not that this situation is confined to Britain. On her cross-national survey Professor Walsh concludes that

There does not appear to be a reservoir of popular enthusiasm awaiting only the institutional means of expression, be these the local elections or participation in boards, committees and meetings. Officials in those cities that have explicitly attempted to increase direct citizen involvement ... have discovered that considerable effort is required to induce people to serve on committees, to form opinions on local issues, and to hold their elected representatives responsible for improving conditions of urban life.[3]

She feels indeed, that the inertia that characterizes the political life of many cities may be due in part to the low incidence of specific demands from 'participants outside the formal political structure'. There may be a lack of opportunity; there probably is a widespread feeling of lack of efficacy – that is, a feeling that the effort of 'participation' would not be worth while because it would not bear fruit.

But even this misses the central point. Most people are not mobilizable for 'political' or community purposes because most of us have a daily round of work, family and recreational preoccupations which consume most of our time, leaving us with little time, inclination or energy for 'politics'. A crisis – the threat of loss of job, home or some valued amenity clearly can cause substantial and effective mobilization. Generally speaking however, the threat has to be perceived as pretty immediate to a sufficiently large group to weld them into a common movement, and there has to be some substantive feeling that common action can bear fruit. These conditions might apply, for example, to the workforce of a factory threatened with closure; or residents threatened with motorway or airport development. They are unlikely to apply in a planning context where citizens feel they are offered a symbolic element of 'participation' unrelated to specific and immediate implications.

The difficulty is further compounded by the different levels at which planning is conducted, such as, on the one hand, the detailed, bricks-and-mortar level of local planning and on the other the general, long-term policy level of structure planning. Thus there are immense potential confusions and frustrations inherent in the situation even without the conflict of values and objectives which the public, the planners and elected representatives are likely to bring into the situation. Nor, of course, should we assume unity in either of these three groups. Much environmental planning involves a conflict for resources and values between the middle and working classes. Then there are conflicts of assumptions, stemming from differing constructions of reality, which may dog communication between planners and the planned. Conservationists and planners might, and often do, stress pollution and noise, traffic and physical decay; a local neighbourhood might see these things as normal and trivial beside the removal of small shops and street corner pubs, distance of travel to decent jobs, facilities for children and teenagers, and so on.

These difficulties would emerge if there were proper mechanisms for effective public participation in planning. We do not, for the most part, yet have them.

In practice, what generally takes place by way of consultation between people and planners today? It varies, of course, but one report, in 1970, from Manchester[4] summed up what no doubt has been a fairly typical situation, prior to very recent years. In the past there had been little or no participation in planning; attempts by either pressure groups or the council to involve people in planning had ended in failure, with the resultant position worse than before in that council officers were unwilling to spend time with pressure groups on future occasions. Public meetings on planning questions only took place when proposals were more or less fixed. Councillors were generally the only direct link between town hall and people. They were pretty poor conductors. They frequently proved incompetent to answer technical questions. Most disliked pressure groups and residents' associations in their wards. (There is indeed a fairly widespread distrust of non-party organizations among local councillors, stemming partly from resentment at the growth of rival non-party, community politics, and in part from genuine puzzlement and scepticism about the new activists' motives – or political sense.) Three years later, in the spring of 1974, in Camden, regarded as one of the more 'enlightened' authorities, a case showed that even there, there was still a long way to go before the case for public participation was treated with proper seriousness. A public meeting was not shown relevant plans concerning the demolition or conversion of a row of buildings, and its overwhelming vote for conversion was ignored by the council's development sub-committee, *despite* the buildings being part of a conservation area with a local advisory committee.[5]

One recent American observer, Stephen L. Elkin, has found the main difference between land-use planning in London and in US cities to be the high degree of insulation of the planning authority in London. There is, he noted, little controversy about who should make decisions, or how, or about what. It is a relatively closed system. The absence of intense overt conflict over land use, in contrast with America, means also that the public officials, though claiming to serve the public interest in land use control, are rarely forced to make explicit statements about public purposes.[6]

There are, it might be suggested, two methods of 'participating' in planning decisions. One is the 'official' way, of quietly utilizing the channels which legislation and the planning authority have made available. This is, as we shall see later, largely a method which leaves initiative, scope and determination in the hands of the authorities. The other method is to take the initiative into one's own hands and conduct a campaign. (The two are not of course exclusive, since any campaigning group of citizens will also want to turn official machinery to their own advantage.)

Antony Jay's *Householder's Guide to Community Defence against Bureaucratic Aggression*[7] presents a formidable outline of the organization and tactics a campaigning citizen group might need to use. He suggests that having established an overall Action Committee, the citizen group should proceed on seven fronts each requiring a specialized small team or cell. These include 'grass-roots' working through neighbourhood representatives; fund-raising; lawyers working on 'enemy' legal errors, unacknowledged citizen rights to be exploited, delaying tactics etc.; 'experts' attacking the concept of the proposal and the facts and figures on which it is based; and so on. Jay is full of valuable advice on how to combat a plan by the production of superior argument, more recent facts and analysis showing how official statistics have been made to lie;

how to exploit doubts and divisions within the official/political hierarchies; how not to alienate potential allies. This is a guide to be inwardly digested by any group of people in potential conflict with 'bureaucratic aggression'. And there is little doubting that this is the way to achieve results. What will be striking immediately, however, is how very middle class, how very London and Home Counties, the list of desiderata is. It is hard to see how the residents of a poor inner urban area can marshal the barrage of experts, publicists and political tacticians Jay's scenario demands.

The point of much of Jay's advice is to enable a prolonged campaign to be mounted, since initial strength of feeling can so easily be worn down by officials using their expertise, not to win every intellectual or moral battle, but to wear down the criticism in a war of attrition. Since loss of face is involved for officials and their political masters, that battle is joined at all is a serious blow to would-be resisters. Much better to try to win the point before public positions are taken up. At the same time, Peter Levin argues that strength of public feeling is, in the last resort, a more vital ingredient than strength of argument.

Under the 'rules of the game' there is less loss of face in a climb-down if it is made in response to strength of feeling than if it acknowledges defeat in argument. Accordingly a demonstration of strength of feeling will provide an opportunity for politicians to reconsider a proposal without necessarily implying that the planners have failed to do their job properly.[8]

Of course, it would be highly desirable if there could be an effective early-warning system to enable strength of local feeling against a proposal to be registered in advance of the drawing of battle lines. And this is the heart of the matter, for, as Jay puts it, 'the crazy thing about protesting is that the time you are most likely to succeed is the time when you are least likely to act. It is at the very beginning of the project that you have the best chance.'[9]

The campaign as a method of participation is likely to have

a continued future no matter what devices are invented to enhance the sensitivity of planning procedures to public opinion. It is a sign that planning is political. Decisions about the allocation of scarce resources are bound to be accompanied by conflict. It is not always right, of course, that a campaign deserves to succeed merely because it is an exercise in public involvement. There is a point at which wider considerations have to be taken into account; such as the balance of interest between those who have campaigned and other interested parties who have not.

One of the greatest difficulties is that gaining and losing in the planning process are different publics (or indeed they could be the same public) who gain or lose at differing degrees of intensity over differing time spans. Bad news is often sudden and affecting a relatively small number of people severely. Beneficial developments often unfold so slowly and effect such masses of people that they are often taken for granted. Motorways are a prime example. The result is that planning proposals are beset by the strong objections of potential losers; while the voice of the more diffused mass of potential beneficiaries is not heard at all. Who is to say which should prevail? Any consideration of participation in planning should bear the latter's claims in mind. Planning should be sensitive to the needs of those most deeply affected by changes. But 'participation' must not be a charter for intense minorities. If it were, it would also be a blueprint for immobilism.

Let us turn now to consider the trend of 'official' thinking in recent years, on means of making opportunities for participation in planning an integral part of the process.

The several years of debate and experimentation following the 1968 Planning Act and the Skeffington Report (1969) may not have brought effective public participation in planning much nearer, but they have illustrated amply the immense difficulties involved in the concept, on the level of democratic theory (whose voices, how much) for planning (the scope and limits of professional competence) and on the operational level (just how is participation organized?). Critics would argue that, for most politicians, and most planners, 'participation' was never *meant* to be more than a bit of window-dressing in response to a vaguely articulated public unease. This may well be so, but it is also the case that no one has come up with an answer to the difficulties.

The 1968 Planning Act provided (a) that adequate publicity should be given to the results of preliminary surveys and to the substance of 'the plan', (b) that persons who may be expected to desire an opportunity of making representations to the authority are made aware that they are entitled to do so; and (c) that they should be given such an opportunity and that the authority should consider any such representations. Like most subsequent proposals and provisions, this concerned the once for all planning decision rather than planning as a continuous process. The provisions could mean as much, or as little, as each planning authority made of them. Any authority sensitive to the need for good public relations would not have done less in an attempt to smooth the way for its plans.

People and Planning[10] published in July 1969, had many good proposals and was full of praiseworthy sentiments. The Skeffington committee felt that the major defect of planning hitherto was failure to communicate. There was a great deal of emphasis on the need for good publicity. They enjoined planning authorities 'not to be unduly touchy or defensive about public criticism or refuse to become involved in public argument'. Continuous open debate would lead to cooperation 'rather than a crescendo of dispute'. To give substance to participation the Skeffington Committee made two main recommendations. 'The yeast of the community' (their words) – the churches, parties, trade unions and voluntary organizations should together form a 'community forum'. It would receive information from the local planning authority, debate alternative courses of action and maintain a dialogue with the planners. It would have its own secretariat. There would be a participants' register, of those wanting to be kept informed. And the committee would cope with the mass of 'non-joiners' by appointing community development officers whose main task would be to develop contacts, and devise means of involving the uninvolved.

The Skeffington Report was largely about means of making the public better acquainted with planning procedures. The initiative was always placed with the local authority. It would have charge of the programme of participation, the surveys of local opinion, and so on. The object of the exercise, patently, was to smooth the path of plans and combat citizen obstructiveness. That obstructiveness might stem not merely from ignorance but also from genuine conflicts of interest, however they might be articulated, did not appear to form part of the committee's consciousness. Instead, the committee relied on goodwill as the solver of problems. Now goodwill is vital in politics, as in all civilized behaviour; but its interests are not best served by its being used to smooth over the cracks, to create a false sense of common purpose.

The community forum was not, on the whole, well received by those intended to be involved in it. They feared emasculation as independent groups. In any case, the problem with any such body of representatives of 'responsible opinion', is how to define criteria for membership. The good, the godly, and the middle class? For the 'non-joiners', that is the vast majority of those likely to be deeply affected by change, yet another caretaker – the community development officer, was proposed. The committee was fuzzy on where his loyalties should lie – and this is a critical weakness in the position of anyone in such a role. To gain the confidence of the underprivileged any such person must be involved with them – but as an employee of the local authority his job would depend on its definition of his effectiveness and not that of the local people. If he were to be really effective as the people's spokesman, it could take a bold authority to stomach him. The Skeffington Committee rather gave themselves away when they asserted that with good publicity and active 'community relations', people should be able to study, discuss and present their views on a particular local plan within 6 weeks of first being informed. Could they have proposed such a brief time if they had seen the main task as anything other than the mobilization of consensus? The proposed public forums, exhibitions, displays of possible 'solutions' have their uses; but more as means of education for participation in planning than as participation itself. They could chiefly be used, after all, simply as devices to ensure for a preconceived plan an easier passage through the political market-place.

The RIBA pointed out,[11] moreover, that the proposals of the Skeffington Committee would not apply to several major types of plan, such as town traffic plans and major road schemes. Major plans would appear only spasmodically, both as regards time and place, while town traffic plans would be implemented 'with far-reaching implications for the whole structure of the environment without any real opportunity for participation at all'. The Ministry of Transport, they pointed out, had required local authorities to submit traffic plans independently of the provisions of the 1968 Act, thus prejudging sensitive issues in a whole range of cases.

Skeffington was hardly greeted with rapture by many involved in the planning scene, especially perhaps the politicians. Many were, understandably, sceptical about participation on the grounds of the criteria of economy, particularly economy of time. These were largely people, however, for whom the countervailing claims of democracy were not at issue since they considered them already catered for.

The weakest argument *against* public participation in planning that came up in the debates on Skeffington was that it would be costly in terms of time. The problem of 'planning blight' – the impact on land, buildings, values and people of uncertainties about possible outcomes has been an acute one; it would stand to reason that the more people involved in decisions, the worse the problem would get. Where citizens and citizen groups have to fight or obstruct to get a hearing, this would certainly be the case. But regulated, built-in participation need not prolong such delays – or inhibit efforts to shorten them. Indeed, the *Architect's Journal* responded to Skeffington by drawing attention to the amount of acrimony and waste of time that could be *saved*. 'Many of the delays caused by public objections and inquiries would be avoided by full public participation at the beginning.'[12]

Skeffington failed to distinguish between public participation and public relations. This was seen in its leaving 'participation' to the final stages rather than at the beginning stage of identifying available choices. As Derek Senior comments, 'from the moment when the planning authority decides which of the available options it prefers, any ostensible consultation of the public falls into the category of public relations'.[13] If public participation in planning is to be anything other than mere public relations, moreover, those wishing to participate must have some resource independent of the politicians and the planners. Lack of access to expertise in developing their case leaves citizens, particularly those already suffering cumulative deprivations, very exposed. Public authorities employ 75 % of planners, while another 20 % are in private practice. Thus few of those with a claim to competence in planning are sufficiently independent of economic and career pressures to be available to plead for those most in need of expert assistance. If there were more who were willing to devote full or spare time to this, the prospects of altering the game might be enhanced.

Meanwhile, new legislation has greatly altered the context in which city planning has taken place. The Town and Country Planning (Amendment) Act of 1972 introduced the 'examination in public' into the development planning system. Structure plans (introduced under the 1968 Act), i.e. those outlining an authority's policy and general proposals, are to be submitted to the Secretary of State, with a statement about the steps that have been taken to publicize the plan and secure public participation, and about the consultations ensuing. Authorities are asked to detail the issues that have emerged, and how they have taken account of views put to them. The Secretary of State has a statutory duty to consider all objections to a structure plan. After due time for dealing with objections, the Secretary of State is to select matters to be examined in public by a small panel with selected participants, including the local planning authority. The matters for discussion are those which should enable the Secretary of State to decide on the plan, and concern broad issues rather than objections as such.

The key concept underlying this is the replacing at structure plan level of the formalized, legalistic inquiry into objections with an intensive but informal discussion by participants who are interested but not necessarily objectors. In selecting participants the basic criterion is 'the effectiveness of the contribution which, from their knowledge or the views they have expressed, they can be expected to make to the discussion of the matters to be examined'.[14] To help them local authorities are asked to give them reasonable access to publishable material, and people with views in common are encouraged to get together beforehand, the better to develop their arguments.

This clearly looks like a vast improvement on the previous system. It implies the recognition that the planning authority is not the repository of all wisdom; that information should be shared; that all relevant issues should be aired, with a view to arriving at the best solution; and that structure planning (though not local planning) should be freed from the restrictive atmosphere of legal detail.

Under the old system, the inquiries were time consuming exercises, not in investigation of the validity of plans themselves, but in defence of affected vested interests. For example, the inquiry into the Greater London Development Plan lasted for most of a year and heard 30,000 objections, even though the plan was couched in deliberately generalized terms. Other advantages of the new concept include the potentiality of freeing of the less specialized participants – such as ordinary citizens affected by possible urban renewal – from the fear of being swept under in a torrent of legal technicalities.

There are, however, worries. The final word is left in the Secretary of State's hands; the examination in public should help ministers to make better decisions but it cannot ensure it. And the minister's responsibility for selecting both participants and issues for discussion gives him great powers. If used insensitively the whole system could be brought into disrepute.

The 'effectiveness of the contribution' criterion favours the articulate, the well organized and the expert. It has been pointed out[15] that 'participation' is far more vague and loose than an 'objection', which does at least have a legal status. Many of the issues, moreover, are too complex and remote for most people to grasp. When the implications of discussions of the public/private capital mix in development, the location and character of transport, shopping and social facilities and so on actually begin to gell into specific bricks and mortar prospects, it will be much later on, in the specific local plans, when it will be too late to object to many of them, since many options will have been foreclosed by the structure plan. Citizen participation *can* only realistically be expected at *this* stage, however, when immediate effects on people's actual, day by day lives begin to become apparent. (This is yet another example of the centrality of the problem for democracy presented by the interaction of different levels of decision-making.)

Hence, one commentator concludes that this new scheme, for all its greater flexibility and apparent responsiveness to the public, will mean *less* participation in planning, especially for the underprivileged. And, he adds,

Perhaps the real loss, in the end, is the credibility of environmental planning itself. For, with the more complex structure plans and the more remote decisions made at public examinations, people will be less interested in exploring and increasing the validity of planning – not more convinced of its value.[16]

Finally, the question remains as to how public (as opposed to expert) participation in structure planning is to be obtained. Debate, research and experimentation here have a long way to go. Nor will they ever be resolved, for they concern little less than the dilemma of democratic citizenship itself.

Various methods of giving effect to the public voice in planning have been tried, with not always very encouraging results. Were people to attempt to produce plans of their own, with expert assistance, this would mean duplicating skills already available in the planning office, and would take a great

195

deal of extra energy. Once again, the criteria of competence and economy emerge; the gain must be worth the candle. Alternatively, the people might be invited to state preferences from a range of 'off-the-peg' plans prepared as alternatives, each designed around the giving of priority, with costs stated, to one value above others. This idea appears both attractive and feasible; though it does carry its penalties. The effort involved in preparation of a *range* of plans is naturally much greater. The plans would have to be simple enough for complete laymen, many with modest education, to understand; yet not so simple as to do injustice to the truth. This would be a delicate task, if not an impossible one. It would be wrong, it might be argued, to ask planners to produce plans to specifications they might disbelieve in for sound reasons, and at the same time to refrain from supporting one rather than another. Nevertheless, this 'shop-window' type of planning activity has clear advantages, particularly in giving an opening to consumer preferences, perhaps especially where a specific local issue, such as the siting of some new amenity, is involved. On a more modified and practicable level, there is the use of a 'choice box' wherein residents can 'spend' counters symbolizing the money to be used for a range of improvements. When residents have 'spent' all their counters the authority has some idea how they would choose as between different improvements. The difficulty here is to ensure that the choices expressed really do represent the majority options of those to be affected.

The most common method of participation is, of course, that whereby people indicate their desires and needs to the planners through their responses to surveys and other methods of opinion elucidation. In any planning procedure the vast bulk of the affected population will not, in all probability, directly participate in any other way. Organization joiners do not lack opportunity to make their views known. But democracy is for everyone. As Bernard Crick has put it, 'it is not enough – although all very liberal, to give people the opportunity to speak up; the views of those who do not speak up must be discovered, cultivated and continuously monitored'.[17]

By survey methods and other means of sociological inquiry we now have means of informing the governmental process with knowledge of how citizens feel and what is important to them. And as Gans has put it 'sociology is a democratic method of inquiry: it assumes that people have some right to be what they are'.[18] In Britain, we have not a good record for taking very seriously the available methods of discovering what people value in their present way of life and desire in order to enhance it. Most local authorities, for example, have been rather inflexible in the past in matching their stock of new housing to the variations in needs, because they have not been geared to the serious study of the profile of those needs as the consumers themselves define them. The whole area of the housing choice, or lack of it, offered to applicants is one case in point. The pressures of supply and demand enter in here, of course, but the local authority has a substantial say in *what* is supplied.

The survey as a method of inquiry is, of course, open to much misuse. Much depends on how questions are framed, how the respondents are chosen, and the use that is made of the results. They can, after all, be used to make it seem that great effort has been expended on, in effect, obtaining popular consent to what would have been done in any case. A more intractable problem is that although planning is about people's futures, naturally, most people find it difficult to give a realistic indication of their reaction to a hypothetical future event, which may not take place, and the consequences of which are a matter for the imagination. People's attitudes to the prospect of moving out of a 'slum' may bear little relation to their attitudes once they have actually moved. Any replies to individual questionnaires administered at one specific point in time may be of questionable meaning.

So merely to conduct surveys is almost certainly not enough. The Town and Country Planning Association has suggested that planning teams should be housed, where possible, in the areas being 'planned' and that the results of surveys, statements of objective, etc. should be published in launderettes, pubs and other places of public resort, so that the crystallization of policy may be enhanced by further discussion. Eversley, among others, suggests[19] that it should be customary for planners to spend time in disadvantaged communities as teachers, aides to social workers, traffic wardens or shop-workers. There was only one *brief* sentence in Skeffington on awareness of the need for public participation as part of the education of planners. More than any quantity of public relations or research technology we need to foster in planning a sense of 'all sorts and conditions of men'; only in encounter with people can that sense grow.

Methods of improving the sensitivity of the planning machinery need to be complemented by improvements in the 'competence' of the planned. For we are talking about a situation of power and powerlessness, of which knowledge of rights and procedures is an important part.

In early 1973 the Town and Country Planning Association started up its Planning Aid Service, with the object of providing information and advice on the workings of the planning system and the rights of the individual within it. The service found in its first year that many people wanted information which the local planning authority should have provided; but they had found the officials unhelpful, or 'often just impatient and unable to explain matters sensibly'.[20] Some simply did not believe what they had been told.

Here is one attempt to balance the scales between the public and the professional planning machine. The TCPA, which can hardly be regarded as a body unsympathetic to planning, argue that though the planning process does have built-in safeguards for the public, these cannot be effective without information and advice on how to use them. The service is restricted to groups, however, whereas it is individuals on their own who are often those most at risk of injury. For these, neighbourhood planning advice centres are needed.

In April 1974 Leeds City Council opened the first 'planning shop' following a recommendation to the government earlier in the year. The idea here is that the authority itself should provide a place with an informal atmosphere akin to a shop, where the citizen can get advice on planning without fear of awesome surroundings or of being shunted about from department to department.

A further hopeful development took place in July 1974 when a private member's bill with all-party support was introduced which would make it a statutory duty for local authorities to notify each individual household in an area which would be affected by the granting of a planning permission. The measure also allowed for tenants' associations to appeal to the government for financial aid towards putting forward a proper case at public inquiries into planning decisions.[21]

The new legislation and techniques have brought us quite some way since Skeffington in recognizing participation in planning as desirable and, indeed, perhaps, as a right. But the achievement in practice is a long way short of the aspiration. Perhaps one reason for the poverty of performance may lie in the absence of recognition of the neighbourhood area as a unit which would speak, in planning, with a voice. What people need is surely a continuing sounding board for their views, which is there whether or not there is an 'issue' pending; and which does not need, therefore, to scramble desperately into existence on an ad-hoc basis when it is nearly too late. More space is devoted elsewhere to this concept. In planning, a neighbourhood council would have considerable potential uses as a sounding board for opinion in relation to both structure and local plans. And it could take its own initiatives in areas at present needlessly removed from local decision. As Cullingworth, indeed, remarks, at street and neighbourhood level 'planners are controlling matters which are of purely local interest and from which they should withdraw'.[22]

Chapter 3 A Role for Media?

That a free and lively press is vital to the health of democracy is a proposition so generally held as to be almost beyond dispute. One of the commonest indicators of authoritarianism in a government is its attitude to the flow of information. Yet clearly there are other ways than governmental fiat, of affecting and indeed controlling, the amount and quality of information in circulation; nor is the disposition of the government itself the only element in the situation. In a free enterprise system Baldwin's charge about the prerogative of the harlot, 'power without responsibility' is justly often laid at the door of those who make a business of disseminating public information, and influencing opinion, for profit. Governments, without necessarily being authoritarian, can be secretive, there are many ways in which they can hinder press efforts to keep the public informed. In order for there to be an effective flow of news and information, there must be on the part of government a willingness to give the fullest of opportunities to the press, and on the press's part the capacity and the incentive to make use of these opportunities.

The press in Britain's cities share certain marked characteristics. Generally speaking each major city has one morning and one evening paper, often produced by the same organization. The evening paper usually is more popular in character, greater in circulation and may well provide a financial crutch for the morning paper. With this monopoly situation, the element of incentive stemming from competition is absent. This is in marked contrast to the situation in the late nineteenth century where in many places there were two or more papers and each political party had its own supportive organ. Moreover, the business of reporting and commenting on local affairs is fraught with peculiar constraints. When so much of what really matters is not decided inside the city at all, and what is left has a heavily administrative and managerial flavour, the local press is inevitably greatly disadvantaged as to local political reporting compared with their national equivalents. The local press has to rely on local interest to carry reader attention through material that might seem to non-locals to be very dull.[1]

It might be argued in defence of the local press that, given these unpromising conditions, they perform their function rather well. Most local papers give a reasonable amount of their non-advertising column-inchage to local government and political affairs, and, lacking an immediate incentive to do so, do it out of a well developed sense of public duty. There is no real evidence of a widespread demand, locally, for a campaigning local press. In so far as the main purposes of a local press are to inform and to entertain, most people can be satisfied on these counts without the press engaging in major, mud-stirring investigations. And if most citizens view local politics, and hence local political news, with an apathetic eye, it would be mistaken to assume that local elected representatives, on the other hand, are all eager to have their work made more difficult by more vigorous local journalism. There is reserve, if not antipathy, on the part of many local authorities and individual members, with regard to the local press. Fear of trivialization and distortion is probably a larger factor than fear of criticism. What councillors often, one suspects, would like from the press is fuller reportage of their own activities and statements, not rigorous democratic debate. In the circumstances, therefore, we might conclude that the local press caters reasonably well for its market, and that, all in all, we have little to complain about.

Yet to take such a view would be to reflect the complacency which often seems pervasive in the world of local public affairs. There are obvious grounds for disquiet. Firstly, on the whole the provincial and local press does not provide a service of sustained criticism of the presumptions, priorities and output of the local politicians and officials. Hence for this reason if for none other, the general tenor of its output tends to be status quo oriented. In the US newspapers are often more of an 'opposition' to government than the 'out' political party. Fleet Street, Colin Seymour-Ure argues,[2] has become in recent years more independent of the political parties as a locus of discussion and criticism. In comparison with either of these cases the role of the British local and provincial press is of distinctly light 'weight'. It is unlikely, in Seymour-Ure's terms, that the latter, unlike Fleet Street, does much political 'agenda-setting'. There is now, following the court cases involving Mr Poulson and former leading personalities in local government in the north-east, a very justified concern about corrupt practices in local government. Yet it is fair to comment that it took legal process, not newspaper investigation, to bring the north-eastern affairs to light. In many such cases, no doubt, a charge of supineness, of lack of desire to investigate or even be critical, could be levelled at the local press. Yet equally clearly this would be to distort the picture. In a letter published in the *Guardian*[3] Mr Harold Evans, the editor of the *Sunday Times* but formerly of the *Northern Echo*, pointed out that a reporter had been put on to investigate the position of leading political figures with regard to local authority contracting, but that he had not succeeded after several months in discovering anything that could be proved. This corroborates the view of Mrs Katharine Graham, chairman of the *Washington Post*, that much of her paper's coverage of Watergate would have been difficult or impossible under British laws. They would have run into the libel laws at every turn. Once anyone had been arrested, they would have been in contempt of court if they had continued to investigate. Mr Evans pointed out, further, that, unlike in America, there are large areas of British public life where no records are available, or where they are they are forbidden to public and press. In particular he mentioned land, property and tax records, all available for inspection in the USA. In this country, therefore, even a newspaper disposed towards investigation, faces daunting obstacles. Even so, good investigatory journalism can be done, provided the *will* to do it is there. Let us cite, for example, the campaign by a Yorkshire newspaper on industrial pollution of the rivers in its area; and the investigations by the *Liverpool Free Press* ('News you're not supposed to know') into the conduct of a city councillor as a landlord of slum properties. Investigation *is* hedged about by legal difficulties, some at least of which spring from a valid desire to protect individual liberties. It is to be hoped that the work of Lord Redcliffe-Maud's committee on corruption in local government will ultimately result in removal of some of these obstacles which at present seem to serve the liberty of the dubious operator better than they do that of the ordinary citizen. At the same time, this might remove some of the excuses behind which, at present, lack of disposition to investigate and campaign can shelter.

Secondly, however, quite apart from investigatory journalism, the *routines* of local government performance are not always covered as well as they might be. There is much reliance on snippets taken from official reports, and verbatim reporting of speeches in council. Fleet Street has many more resources than Hansard and official government publications. In particular, it has its lobby correspondents and its free-ranging political columnists. The local political scene does not offer the same scope, and the smaller local paper, particularly the weekly, does not, often, have the staff in any case. Thus many newspapers are *more* dependent on the council for their material than was the case, say, 60 years ago. If a plurality of sources is essential to democratic debate, this situation must be very much regretted.

Thirdly, much of what is reported inevitably misses the neighbourhood dimension within which much of the citizen–town hall interface takes places. The field of surveillance is likely to be the whole city, and space and the tolerance of other readers, will hardly permit one area 'hogging' the news, though no one would, no doubt, object to the odd campaigning cover given to a particular group of residents and their problems, especially if these can be generally identified with.

Since much of this situation inheres in the structure of city government/provincial press relationships, action to improve the situation ought not to be left to the existing media working on their own. We have already mentioned legal considerations inhibiting investigations of some types. There is also a general British passion for secretiveness in government. The press can attend council meetings and committee meetings now, but all exclusions, where possible, should be given a public justification, and there ought to be some means of effective sanction on persistently secretive local authorities.[4] There may be scope for educational work enabling councillors and officials on the one hand and journalists on the other to become more closely acquainted with each other's problems and requirements. There are training schemes in existence at present for junior journalists, but some of their seniors are somewhat sceptical as to the efficacy of these. Means might be explored of encouraging newspaper groups to employ specialist columnists on city government affairs, who could go beyond the handouts, official papers and committee minutes, and whose expertise would be sufficient to defend them against being unwittingly 'incorporated' into the town hall point of view.

None of these things will however have more than a marginal effect on life down in the grass roots. Here, arguably, is where a new departure is needed most. The growth in recent years of a community press is sometimes seen as an 'alternative' to the existing local press. It may well be that 'alternative' methods are employed, or that those active in its promotion have links with that loose and incoherent syndrome known as the 'alternative society'. But to think of a 'community' press as alternative to the provincial daily press is as false as to see the latter as an 'alternative' to Fleet Street. They are different horses on different courses. There is considerable room for experiment with a neighbourhood press, produced by local people, and the photolithographic techniques developed in recent years enable a paper of limited run and circulation of, say, 6,000 (which seems to be the upper limit of most of them) to be a viable proposition. Such a paper and any form of neighbourhood council would, normally, be mutually supportive, though it would be unnecessarily stifling of experiment to prescribe any fixed pattern. Financial aid for the starting or maintaining of such a project might come direct from the neighbourhood council or from any other source that might be funding both.

Mention should be made of the possibilities of local radio, and, in the future, perhaps of cable TV. Clearly the scope for debate and the imparting of information is substantial; yet as a tool for participation the search for a viable formula is a difficult one.[5] There is obvious scope for experiment in the broadcasting of council debates (or edited highlights), or the meetings of tenants' associations, civic societies or neighbourhood councils. People will surely welcome the chance to hear themselves and their friends and neighbours talk. The greatest difficulty is probably that of coping with the relationship between the tiny minority of experts or insiders and the rest of the population, the nature of whose contribution to a programme cannot be predicted in advance. Here, too, we are not only dealing with two (at least) sets of people, the ordinary citizens and the decision-makers, but also with a third, the media personnel themselves, who will be working according to their own criteria of effective broadcasting. 'Access broadcasting' by citizen groups given their own air-time, may help to ease this difficulty, but a layman remains a layman in the world of media no less than in that of planning or housing or education. Creating scenarios for effective communication and citizen participation in decision-making presents problems as likely to be thrown into greater relief by broadcasting as to be resolved by it.

Chapter 4 Parish Councils for Cities?

> *... in the world of local community action and politics we have not exhausted the capacity for innovation which created trade unions, political parties and other institutions, once regarded as subversive, that are now recognised by the law and incorporated in statutory decision-making procedures.*
>
> – David Donnison[1]

> *... think about appropriate units of democracy as an ascending series, a set of Chinese boxes, each larger and more inclusive than the other, each in some sense democratic, though not always in quite the same sense, and each not inherently less nor inherently more legitimate than the other.*
>
> – Robert A. Dahl[2]

Introduction: general considerations

The city is citizens. Both words come from a common root. Yet it is clear that our inherited language and concepts of democracy are mocked by the sheer scale and complexity of the way we live in cities now. The Athenian polis would have failed, by far, even to qualify as a metropolitan borough. So would every British city, except London, two centuries ago. The genie is out of the box; and answers to the problem of citizenship which might have been valid in times past will suffice no longer.

If we are to forge a tolerable future for our urbanized society we cannot evade the responsibility for using accumulations of political power and resource appropriate to the scale and complexity of the difficulties. The temptation to suppose that we can do otherwise appears, however, to be strong. Some sensitive people appear attracted by an anarchist or utopian urge to hark back to notions of 'community' based on misperceptions of the human society of earlier generations. Nevertheless, the richness that ought to be implied in the idea of self-government, of citizenship, is thinned away into poverty by the widespread feeling, and the fact, of individual powerlessness in our society.

It is surely a legitimate activity of political analysts and activists to explore means of cherishing that self-government, that citizenship.

Power should be placed in the hands of the smallest unit that is capable of satisfactorily coping with the public's business. This begs some very large questions. But if it means that we have to live with large scale units for policy-making, it also means we ought to see whether there is a role for units of power considerably smaller than those that have existed in present times in the cities. If we apply to city life the principle of maximum feasible power for minimum feasible areas we arrive at the concept of the neighbourhood council, the common council, the urban parish council. The name hardly matters. What does, is the principle – that at the level of most primary interactions, the home district, citizens should have as much of a voice, as much power to adapt local services to local circumstances and needs, as may be compatible with the claims of the wider city.

The case for the urban parish council has to be carefully made, for its critics can put up a formidable range of objections. Some would say, and correctly, that the whole gallimaufry of 'community politics' threatens to be a frivolous distraction of attention from the serious business of running the multimillion pound enterprise that is urban government today. Two tiers of urban government as well as the national government, are complicated enough to run. Adding yet another is no simple matter.

We have, in addition, a great variety of evidence to consider. There is the long-established practice of parish government outside the large towns. There is the evidence of how people inside the cities view their local situation. There is the evidence of what has happened where some experiments have already taken place in establishing non-statutory councils in the big cities. And so on.

Let us pause first, however, to dispose of a fallacy. That

what we are talking about has anything, except in the vaguest sense, to do with 'community'.

No term which might have had a useful role to play has been more beaten into senselessness than 'community'. And especially so when what is meant is a small section of a city. Much of the difficulty arises because the idea of 'community' has a remarkably wide appeal. It has an honoured place in both the conservative and the socialist traditions in political thought. 'I believe', writes Robert Nisbet, 'that community is the essential context within which modern alienation has to be considered.'[3] In this sense, the word implies a high degree of solidarity based upon common interests, experiences and relationships. Tonnies's *Gemeinschaft* was community based on kinship, locality or friendship. But he contributed to the debasing of the term by using it to characterize an entire form of society, setting it over against *Gesellschaft*. The relationship between 'community' in this sense and a particular locality within a city is fairly remote. To most citizens, their family, work, recreational and other interests have much more to do with their relationships than the territory of their residence. An area *may* be inhabited by people sharing similar values, but for the most part these are likely to relate to sources external to the locality as such. Many people in cities, particularly the more mobile, are members of, at best, what Pahl calls a 'community of limited liability', where they may exercise many freedoms not open to the lifelong inhabitant of, say, a small country town, knowing that when they leave the area they take their social mistakes with them. Those who bemoan the loss of 'community' do not emphasize the involuntary commitments, the pressures on the non-conforming, the lack of means of wiping slates clean, that tend also to be part of the package.

When the word is used to refer to an area within a city, as in 'community politics', 'the community press', 'community action', the term has gained such wide recognition that it would be pedantic to avoid it altogether. But it is important to realize (as many people evidently do not), that 'mere living together in the same locality can result in a conglomeration of very little sociological importance'.[4] The validity of new forms of neighbourhood political life in cities does not depend upon 'community'. The concept introduces an element of mystification we are better off without.

Parish councils in practice

Political units of neighbourhood size have existed *outside* the cities in Britain for centuries. 'In many parts of the country', in Derek Senior's view, 'they have been by far the most vital and satisfying form of local democracy.'[5] Although to write of 'parish councils' in the context of political renewal in cities may seem like calling in the old world to the redress of the new, a glance at their performance is worthwhile. Old as they are, they are uniquely of the neighbourhood, they have resources and the capacity to use them, and they have functioned for a very long time as a lower tier in our system of representative government.

Up to the mid nineteenth century, parish government largely *was* local government, covering about five sixths of the population of the country – all, in fact, except the chartered towns. The parishes, with the poor law to administer, raised and spent about one fifth of the sum spent by the national government. Today, many may be tempted to dismiss the parish council as a bucolic institution appropriate only for scattered rural districts. And it is true that of the 9,954 parishes in England and Wales in existence at the time of the Redcliffe-Maud Report, 44 % had populations of less than 300. But this represents only a relatively small proportion of people living in parishes. Much more common was the citizen living in a suburb, large village or in 'industrial' countryside. And it is the more urban parishes, and those in the more industrial counties, which were the more lively, measured in terms of both of their financial and their electoral activities. An exception to this generalization was the highly rural Cambridgeshire and the Isle of Ely. Cambridgeshire of course, has in its village colleges, a system which predates recent thinking on the 'community school' by decades. Cambridgeshire and Ely were among the handful of counties where each parish council was notified of planning applications affecting its area, and encouraged to comment. By 1970, some 7,000 parishes in England and Wales had a functioning council, the rest being small and having only parish meetings. Although operating under a constant threat of erosion, as successive local government acts strengthened the hand of the higher tier authorities, nevertheless the parish councils were capable of attracting a degree of enthusiasm often lacking in the higher tiers. In 1970 Jane Morton wrote that 'by all the indices the parish sector is now about the healthiest part of the local government system. In the last 10 years, expenditure has grown at a faster rate than local government expenditure as a whole. It's a rare year when there is not at least one new council formed.'[6] And with 57,000 seats, parish councils enabled more people to participate in government than any other tier of the governmental system.

Parish councils have no statutory duties. All their powers are permissive. They have no services to administer and large blocs of public funds are not involved. If this means their powers are limited, it also means they are free to be flexible and unbureaucratic. They may precept for a small rate (now 2p) on their own initiative, may levy a higher rate with the approval of the annual parish meeting, while the minister retains a veto over still larger ones. The Local Government Act of 1963 allowed the expenditure of a 'free fifth'; that is, $\frac{1}{5}$d. (old pence) for the good of the parish to be spent on anything that could not be provided in any other way. Thus, the parish councils do have a resource, if limited, and the power that goes with it. In 1964–5, larger councils spent between £2,000 and £14,000, chiefly on street lighting (33 %) and the provision of playing fields and other recreational facilities (23 %). The 'free fifth' was spent on such things as Citizens' Advice Bureaux, anti-litter campaigns, prizes for best kept allotments, and similar minor aids to better-quality living. The money might be small (although so too is the cost to the citizen) but the capacity for taking initiatives within the permitted framework is limited only by the shape of demand and the imaginations of parish councils. Because of this they form a good, if hitherto largely ignored, set of examples of what an urban neighbourhood might do if given the capability.

A survey (for the Redcliffe-Maud Commission)[7] of 8 parish councils in Oxfordshire and the West Riding demonstrated not only how they used their initiatives in spending to meet purely local needs but also how they functioned as a neighbourhood level tier in an interlocking network of local government.

Individual styles of expenditure included Ackworth's (population 4,089) purchase of a former doctor's surgery for use as a pensioners' recreation room; or Boston Spa's (population 2,426) spending £1,500 on two tennis courts, as well as a sum of £15 to £20 on bus shelters, footpaths, and planting of trees and flowers. The councils also used their money to help themselves to function as focal points for the building and maintenance of community facilities such as halls, and the provision of assistance to voluntary associations. Parishes, it is estimated, sustain in various ways some 70,000 such associations. The parish hall at Chipping Camden[8] for instance, is used by some 40 local organizations.

But it is perhaps the potential role of the councils in consumer representation to the service providing authorities which is of most significance. For instance, 239 West Riding parishes between them had made 1,000 representations about the state of the roads in a period of 2 years. They were in touch with 6 government departments and 7 public bodies, such as the National Coal Board. In the West Riding and Oxfordshire, in fact, 80% of the councils had made representations about traffic management; many had taken up with the higher authority such local issues as the hours of library opening and the placing of unsightly overhead cables. Boston Spa, again, assisted the County Council in a survey of every house in the parish, and after a lengthy altercation, succeeded in getting the Rural District Council to refer all planning applications to it for comment. The National Association of Parish Councils estimated that consultation of some sort took place in two thirds of the rural districts. The Cambridgeshire County Council itself notified all parishes of planning applications and requested replies within 15 days, so that notification did not entail delays in reaching decisions. In Oxfordshire, applicants to the County for planning permission sent a summary of their application to the parish council concerned which could then make its comments. The authors of the research report on the 8 Yorkshire and Oxfordshire parish councils concluded that:

Despite limited powers, the wide range and considerable extent of activity found in these eight parishes is the overwhelming point to emerge from this brief survey. It is important to bear in mind that all of these activities are voluntary, for the parish council powers are all permissive. In this sense level of activity is largely a reflection of spontaneous demand, and it is interesting to note that most activities lie in the direction of providing better amenities for the community and representing its collective interests before other public authorities.[9]

It is indeed hard to see why the opportunity for such patently fruitful activity should be available to some citizens but denied to the great urban majority. As the experience of the existing parish councils suggests, the real question of local neighbourhood power is not primarily a financial one – the sums they could dispose of independently of wider policy-making cannot conceivably be great, although they might make a great difference to a small locality. Nor is it primarily representational. A sheer increase in the number of representatives would hardly, in itself, be a significant improvement. More to the point is the ability of a really active parish council to counterbalance the concentration of power at the centre. This in two ways. First, by enabling all kinds of local activity to have a firm local focus, thus encouraging local self-help, and strengthening the client end of the centre-field axis along which service provision is conducted. Secondly, by providing a local body with the right to be informed and comment on the policy coming from the centre, and hence, it may be hoped, to force the political leadership, the professionals and the bureaucrats to make more explicit and if need be defend the grounds on which their proposals rest. In other words, not to remove policy-making from the centre (that would almost certainly lead to highly undesirable consequences) but to make it more sensitive to the definition of the situation at the point of impact.

The Redcliffe-Maud Commissioners approved the existing parish councils, indeed proposing that the willingness of local inhabitants to sanction spending in their name should be the only financial limitation on them. They suggested that outgoing boroughs and urban districts might join them in the same powers and functions under the new order. They did acknowledge, however, that 'people may prefer to substitute councils representing neighbourhoods'.

The principle was recognized in the subsequent Act, but only as regards the former local government units which were allowed to transmute their former councils into urban parish councils with rather vague functions. Otherwise there was no obligation laid on the newly established local authorities to create urban parish councils, even if there was popular demand for them. The Conservative government's preference was to let the new system settle down with the possibility of going into the parishes question in the 1980s. But Scotland, which had not had parish councils for 45 years, was to have them again where 20 or more citizens locally asked for one. London, its government reorganized a decade earlier than the rest of the country, was in a different position again, with no provision or promise of provision at all. In 1973–4 a Liberal-sponsored London Parish Councils Bill gained substantial support in an effort to extend to London's boroughs the right to set up statutory rate spending urban parish councils.

In a speech in February 1974, however, Mr Harold Wilson agreed that such councils 'would be a vital step in making democracy articulate. For, if democracy means choice, that choice has to be so close to the individual that he can identify and express the issues on which he cares deeply and having identified and expressed, to choose.' In October 1974 the government circulated an exploratory document indicating that it considered the time ripe for further action, but subsequently the proposal was shelved. (Confusion in the new system was probably to blame. The top tier metropolitan counties are widely unpopular and felt to be purposeless.)

How, then, should the urban parish be constituted, how should its boundaries be set, what should it do? Let us consider some further evidence.

Mini-government: an American case

The American metropolitan scene often appears to be one of democracy gone mad. In no country has suburbanization gone so far; and at the same time no country has, as part of its central political ideology, such a fiercely guarded belief in local self-government. As a result, each metropolitan area has been made up of perhaps hundreds of local government units, all independent as far as key areas of politics such as land use and local taxation are concerned. By 1957, for example, 174 metropolitan areas containing 108 million people, had 15,678 separate governmental jurisdictions. Greater New York had 1,400 of them.[10] The patent ungovernability of America's great metropolitan complexes has led to moves, successful in some cases, to create one single metropolitan government. 'Going metro' may be, in one sense, an escape from the awful consequences of too much grass-roots democracy. But it is better to see it simply as a logical and necessary move to fit the governmental system more closely to the facts of life in the large city. Most schemes for 'going metro' recognize the validity of a lower tier of government, and some, of a neighbourhood tier. One such is the experiment in 'mini-government' which was part of the recent scheme of metropolitan government for greater Indianapolis.[11] Some of its provisions probably reflect the need to overcome local resentment at incorporation in a metropolitan jurisdiction; and some, as we shall see, have a distinctly American flavour to them, which one would hardly urge for Britain.

Recent legislation in Indiana provided for the division of cities into communities of not less than 5,000 persons. A Metropolitan Development Commission, established in 1971, was empowered to prepare a plan taking into account a range of factors in delineating community boundaries – the boundaries that might be formed by major roads, railways and water-courses; boundaries of school districts; retail trading patterns; existence and extent of community and neighbourhood associations; as well as historical political boundaries. Each community so defined was empowered to decide by referendum to establish an elective Community Council, and to acquire rights and powers accordingly. We note elsewhere the problems of what to do about party politics in urban parish councils. Indiana makes it illegal for parties to endorse Community Council candidates, or for candidates in any way to advertise a political affiliation. There is a Community Fund with monies placed to its credit by the city, and the Council gets a share of revenues distributed by the state. The City Council may designate for local use part or all of the state taxes on motor fuel, tobacco, etc. The Community Council can contract with the city for community improvements and recreational facilities. It can regulate car parking and vehicle movement on roads not designated as county thoroughfares, subject to higher, i.e. City Transportation Board, approval. In turn, it receives notice of any proposals regarding thoroughfares in its area and has time to submit comments on them. At any time it can propose amendments of the city's Master Plan to the Metropolitan Development Commission and will receive technical assistance from them in presenting its amendments. It is entitled to represent any of its residents before, and be heard as an interested party in, any proceeding affecting the community or its residents held by city agencies and departments. Finally, it can hire auxiliary police protection, subject to general city police approval.

Senior on common councils

Derek Senior, in his memorandum of dissent to the Redcliffe-Maud Report, made perhaps the most lucid case for parish councils in cities, or, as he chose to call them, 'common councils', being an English equivalent of the continental 'commune'. The council's primary function, as Senior saw it, would be to be a sounding board for community views. It would not run statutory services, but 'it would be able to exert a positive influence on the way statutory services were run within its area'.[12] Those responsible for running the services would have the duty to inform it, consult it, and take account of its comments. It would have power to spend on amenities as much money as local ratepayers would permit, provided it did not infringe on the statutory duties of other governmental tiers, or exceed sums allocated in regional investment programmes. The common council should nominate to school governors and managers – indeed they should have a majority of local members, and naturally they would have representation on other bodies operating in their areas, such as transport users' councils and amenity bodies.

Many able people who would not consider the political and administrative work of district or county councils may be willing to do a turn at the parish pumps. Hence, Senior argues, the urban parish council, or common council, cannot come into its own unless it is seen from the outset as quite different in kind from the service-running local authority, and the roles of the two must be incapable of being confused. For electoral purposes boundary lines will have to be made somewhere, but it will hardly matter greatly if the spheres of activity engaged in have, at the edges, fuzzy territorial referents. If it is to be an effective unit, argues Senior, it should emerge (with encouragement) from the pre-existent pattern of residents' feelings, rather than being imposed on them.

It is of the essence of the common council concept that where the sense of community is not strong enough to give rise to a demand for a common council there should be no need to have one. Conversely, every community which recognises itself as such should be entitled and encouraged to have a common council.[13]

The existence of a community association would be the best available test of ripeness for the emergence of a council, thinks Senior, though it would be wrong simply to give an existing voluntary community organization the power of a parish council to levy a rate. If the existence of local feelings is the criterion, a wide range of sizes of area should be accepted. This would accommodate the finding of the Redcliffe-Maud Community Attitudes Survey[14] that while in the conurbations and other larger cities, for most people 'home' is the group of roads within a ten-minute walk of the place of residence, in the smaller boroughs people may identify with the whole town.

Drawing the line somewhere

The neighbourhood in a city is a concept which most people recognize as having, for them, a definite meaning. The Community Attitudes Survey confirmed that 78 % of electors hold in their mind a 'mental map' of the city in which there is a distinct 'home territory' to which they feel a peculiar attachment. For most, this was an area no larger than an average pre-1972 Act ward. 80 % of people had friends living within 10 minutes' walk. Of course, no two households will share identical 'home territories'. Only an imperfect definition of a 'home area' is provided by such institutions as churches, pubs, schools and shopping-centres. Their salience varies from area to area and from household to household. Nor is attachment to a local area equally powerful amongst the social classes. The survey found that the groups most likely to show strong area attachment were the less educated, the lower socio-economic grades and those living nearer to the centres of towns. In confirming this, Hampton's survey in Sheffield[15] found an even higher proportion, 85 %, who recognized a 'home area'. Of these, three-quarters described a very small territorial mental map, mentioning just a few streets surrounding their address.

Another survey, conducted by Michael Young and the National Suggestions Centre in Hornsey,[16] a part of the Greater London Metropolitan Borough of Haringey, attempted to collate people's mental maps, to provide a reasonably coherent picture. There emerged, in Hornsey, 10 neighbourhood areas, with populations of 6 to 12 thousand, i.e. rather smaller than most pre-1972 wards, and implying as many as 800 in the whole GLC area, or around 65 in Liverpool or Manchester.

Another approach to the problem of definition is to see just how much is 'given' by the existing pattern of administrative sub-division in a city. An exploration of this in Sheffield[17] found that the (pre-1972 Act) ward was too large, having populations well in excess of say, a viable notional number of 10,000 people. But the polling districts were appropriate sized. Most of us may not know their boundaries, but the political activists do and so does the administration. Moreover, they have centres which might be potential locations for activities. The same goes for school catchment areas, and, of course, school–community relations are an important field which urban parish councils might develop. In this case, though, the boundaries are less clear. Sheffield also uses residential area units for development control purposes. Using these 3 divisions, polling districts, school areas and residential areas, it was found that the degree of coincidence of these is fairly substantial, and covers 390,000 of the 540,000 inhabitants of the city, in 65 discernable neighbourhood units. Definition is weakest in the inner areas, though here railways and future urban motorways may contribute to demarcation.

In Hornsey,[18] three-quarters of citizens questioned favoured the idea of neighbourhood council, especially on the grounds of 'bringing things down' to the local scale. Half had 'topics' for it to take up.

% of total sample mentioning each topic

Roads, parking, public transport	20%
Services for old people	12%
Schools	11%
Housing	9%
Refuse collection and street cleaning	6%
Health and welfare	5%
Open space, leisure facilities	4%

Preoccupations no doubt vary from place to place. In many areas the whole field of traffic and highways may be felt as one where the neighbourhood is made to suffer unduly for the convenience of people external to it; hence the call for some redress of the balance. In many of the inner areas most at the receiving end of urban change, the evidence from the Sheffield survey suggests that high neighbourhood attachment may be unassociated with high consciousness, as gauged by knowledge of the city's political institutions; and that this would be both a great problem for a neighbourhood council, and a justification for building something at the level where events *have* meaning and interest is high.

The neighbourhood councils

In recent years a considerable movement for the development of urban neighbourhood councils of one kind or another has grown up. They have varied greatly in their styles of organization and political postures and have met with varying degrees of success. Some, such as the Golborne Neighbourhood Council in North Kensington, have been highly controversial from the start. In general the councils have grown up outside the local government system and have had, as a key issue, the problem of what kind of relationship they should have with the local city or borough council. This has involved questions of political tactics, of resources, and of legitimacy. There is no single resolution of the ambiguities the councils have found themselves enmeshed in. It is largely a matter of deciding what kind of body each wants to be.

In Liverpool there were by the early 1970s between a dozen and 20 neighbourhood councils, operating with varying degrees of effectiveness. Generally, they were run by executive committees of 24 members elected by an annual meeting. They grew up independently of the city council and relations between them were slow to develop, there being considerable caution on each side about the other. On the other hand, 10 councils in Lambeth arose directly through initiatives taken by the Labour controlling group at Town Hall, though only for the minority of areas where they were wanted. Making their own constitutions they hence showed a variety of forms and also of activities. Some were much stronger 'demanders' of the borough council than others. The Lambeth councils were elected at public meetings. In Toxteth, Liverpool, by contrast, elections for the community council were held early in 1973 on a street and block constituency basis; turn-out was 50 %, a notable achievement in a city whose overall turn-out at local, city council elections, had varied, over the previous 5 years, from 28·5 % to 36·4 %, with much lower figures in the inner area. It appears that a firm grounding in a street and block basis is the best basis for success. Critics have argued that Golborne in North Kensington, lacked this. The failure of the experiment there, which ran into difficulties after an initially encouraging start, shows, incidentally, the importance of constitutions. If they are got wrong, the venture may fail. The neighbourhood council must be both representative and effective, to gain support; and this means extreme care in constructing it, both constitutionally and in terms of action. Certainly, the fact that the Golborne council experiment did not succeed need not be taken as pointing to inevitable failure for the idea of a neighbourhood council. For one thing, North Kensington has been for several years something of a hotbed of experiment in 'community action'. It might have been expected that frictions between personalities, and particularly between 'residents' and full-time activists and 'outsiders' would develop. Again, it controlled no resources and hence had no formal political powers. There were ambiguities in the neighbourhood council's relationship to the local government system on the one hand and the people of the area on the other.

Any do-it-yourself neighbourhood council is going to be in a rather anomalous or ambiguous relationship with both the local authority and the local people. One solution would be to make a virtue out of the lack of formal political powers and create a body free of all local authority entanglements and able to act as a free-ranging watchdog and pressure-exerting body. This is the view of many of the more militant 'community activists', who want a council whose keynote would be flexibility. It would incorporate local action and pressure groups, would relate to 'street groups' and so on. It would not be hamstrung by the procedures of conventional democracy.

But this would be a solution not without its price. Such a council would still be resourceless, and it would be cut off from the local government system which, like it or not, has the resources and the powers. It would be limited in its power to employ expertise. And it would have no legitimacy. No one, resident or councillor or official, would be obliged to pay it any more attention than he would to any other self-appointed group of 'spokesmen'.

In conclusion

Should, then, the neighbourhood or parish councils be a statutory tier of the local government system, or not? Although there are good reasons against, those for are better. The chances of making the system more sensitive to local needs and definitions of the situation would seem greater when those local definitions are expressed by a body with constitutionally recognized standing, and resources, even though from time to time this might be at some cost in freedom and flexibility. Nor, in any case, are we talking about an either/or situation. Any group of people is still free to set up its own body to exert its own influence, for what that is worth.

Certainly the answer to the question of how effective a council can be in mobilizing action, and how seriously politicians and administrators will take it, is likely to vary from place to place, and hence too should the form of the council. There is much to be said for retaining as much flexibility as possible. It should not be foisted on local people who do not want it. Rural parish councils operate to the same principle. And it is well if the basic form and procedure is evolved by local people and not imposed on them from without. Within these considerations, however, the urban parish council would benefit from having a permanent constitutionally accepted status.

One of the most difficult things to decide is the degree of local initiative that would warrant the setting up of a council. Upswellings of 'community' feelings may arise from place to place and from time to time, but it would be unwise to bank too much on the prospect. The potentiality that an elected neighbourhood council might itself encourage a local sense of identity and local action, should not be overlooked. The relationship between constitutional arrangements and political orientations is not entirely a one-way process. If the concept is intrinsically of value, perhaps it ought not to be hazarded to an entirely optional process. The evidence on participation, as we have seen, should provide a warning there.

To work properly, the system would need to be properly financed, even though in relative terms the money involved would be small. By the early 1970s existing parish councils spent about £5 million p.a., or 0·1 % of the total local government bill for England and Wales. In the first instance, and like the parish councils at present, the new ones might levy a small local rate. Secondly, they might have the capacity for raising loans or holding lotteries for specific projects such as social or recreational centres, which might ultimately be expected largely to pay for themselves. Thirdly, some of the monies which would be spent in any case by higher authorities might simply be redirected. Block grants or grants for specific uses could be utilized here. Block grants can be used to combat the disparities between the privileged and under-privileged areas, in that they can be fixed on a rateable value basis. Where, Michael Young suggests, the average block grant might be £1 per head, it could range in practice from 50p to £1.50 depending on the measures of need adopted. Fourthly, there is the possibility of hypothecation to the neighbourhood council of a portion of annual local authority income. Since the greatest obstacle to popular consent might well arise from the notion that the council should be empowered to spend any monies they could persuade their constituents to sanction, hypothecation, or a block grant system, would be a way to get round it.

If the system is to be an accepted part of our democratic machinery, considerable care would need to be exercised over the method of election and representation. For instance, the question of whether or not party politics should be permitted is bound to arise. We have seen that in the Indianapolis scheme, party labels are not allowed. We have to acknowledge that there is a widespread dislike of party politics in local government, and many people no doubt might be deterred if parish elections were to be fought on party lines. Political parties, for all their faults, however, are collectivities which can be made to stand for something and be held responsible for their stewardship. They care about power. Representatives elected in an explicitly non-partisan election may not care whether they are re-elected or not (there is some evidence that suggests this) and hence may not be subject to the pressure of popular opinion. In any event, this is a question which is probably best left to local opinion.

Constitutionality and flexibility – these are the central requirements of an effective neighbourhood council system for cities. Methods of election, representation, boundaries, resource provision, terms of office need to be carefully devised. But the ultimate form of council life must be flexible enough to be able to assume the shape of the neighbourhood's needs and preoccupations. The system, more than any other, would depend for its success on the mobilization of such widespread support that there should be as little room as possible for the charge that the neighbourhood council was not, after all, a legitimate institution for the neighbourhood or an effective agent for the promotion of its interests. In so saying, we are only really prescribing for the urban neighbourhood that concept of association of citizens for the purpose of self-government which is what democracy is all about.

A note on redress of grievances: the local ombudsman

In April 1967, the British Ombudsman, or, officially, Parliamentary Commissioner for Administration, took up office. This investigator of citizens' complaints into maladministration now has an accepted, useful if undramatic, role to play in the relationship between the citizen and central government. M Ps, through whom access to the ombudsman is channelled, have found, however, that a high proportion of complaints received could not be transmitted to the ombudsman because they concerned local government. This is in itself further indication of local government's importance as a source of governmental impacts on peoples' lives.

It had long been recognized that ombudsmen for local government would be a logical extension of the concept.[19] The 1974 Local Government Bill provided for local ombudsmen located in various regional centres. While this may be welcomed, it should be seen as a basis on which to build rather than a completed task. For the system appears rather weak. Weaker indeed than that which has been operating in Northern Ireland since 1969. The English commissioners do not report to Parliament, but to representative bodies of local authorities. Complaints must be channelled through councillors, just as those to the national ombudsman must go through MPs. Both of these provisions weaken the ombudsman as a critic of maladministration. It is hard to see that the status of MPs would be seriously undermined by direct public access to the ombudsman's office; as regards councillors, the situation is rather more problematic, but the effective defence of citizens against bureaucratic blunders has a higher value, surely, than the preservation in its entirety of this particular aspect of the councillor's role. Finally, what happens if the ombudsman does find that injustice has been done? The Northern Irish ombudsman can try to settle the issue himself, and can make recommendations to local authorities for future practice, while the citizen may, in the last resort, seek compensation in court. In England if the local ombudsman is not satisfied with a local authority's attitude, there is not much he can do about it except make another public report.

Stacey[20] considers that the parliamentary commissioner's impact has been muted by the limitations of scope imposed upon him. At present it seems likely that the same may be said of the local ombudsmen. However, once an institution is in being, it can be strengthened. The local ombudsman may well have more work to do than the national. Given decent publicity and a willingness by councillors and citizen groups, through them, to press cases, here is a small but valuable new weapon against bureaucratic ineptitude or worse. Sir Edmund Compton considers that as Parliamentary Commissioner he had 'a general tonic effect'[21] on government departments (even where actual cases of maladministration had not been proven). At the very least, we may hope his local equivalents to have the same. Whether they have *more* will probably depend upon whether their prospective degree of toothlessness so destroys interest that no one bothers to press for ameliorative dentistry.

References

For brevity's sake only major references have been included.
1 The quotations at the front of the book and in the preface are from Theodore Lowi's *The End of Liberalism*, Norton, 1969 p. 272.

Part One

Chapter One

1 Quoted in Read, Donald, *Documents from Edwardian England*, Harrap, 1973, p. 20.
2 Rodwin, Lloyd, *Nations and Cities*, Houghton Mifflin, 1970, p. 153.
3 Quoted in Weber, A. F., *The Growth of Cities in the Nineteenth Century*, Macmillan, 1899.
4 Dyos, H. J. (ed.), *The Study of Urban History*, Edward Arnold, 1968, p. 40.
5 Pahl, R. E., *Patterns of Urban Life*, Longman, 1970, p. 17.
6 Geddes, Patrick, *Cities in Evolution*, revised ed. Williams and Norgate, 1949, p. 26.
7 Cobbett, William, *Rural Rides*, Penguin, 1967, p. 216.
8 Dyos, H. J., *Victorian Suburb*, Leicester University Press, 1961, p. 19.
9 See White, B. D., *History of the Corporation of Liverpool*, Liverpool University Press, 1951.
10 Quoted Dyos, H. J., op. cit., 1961, p. 52.
11 Dyos, H. J. and Wolff, M., *The Victorian City: Images and Realities*, vol. II, Routledge & Kegan Paul, 1973, p. 893.
12 See e.g. Kellett, J. R., *The Impact of the Railways on the Victorian Cities*, Routledge & Kegan Paul, 1969.
13 Dyos, H. J., op. cit., 1961, p. 23.
14 Kellett, J. R., op. cit., 1969, p. 294.
15 ibid., p. 290–305.

16 Chapman, S. D. (ed.), *The History of Working-Class Housing*, David & Charles, 1971.

17 Wohl, A. S., 'The Housing of the Working Classes in London 1815–1914', in Chapman, S. D., op. cit., pp. 15–43.

18 See 'Profile of the Conurbations', *Royal Commission on Local Government in England* (Cmnd 4040), vol. III, *Research Appendix 4*, pp. 57–75.

19 See Jones, E., *A Social Geography of Belfast*, Oxford University Press, 1960.

20 See Hall, Peter, 'The Development of Communications', in Coppock, J. T. and Prince, H. C., *Greater London*, Faber, 1964.

21 See Stevens, D. F., 'The Central Area of London', Coppock, J. T. and Prince, H. C., op. cit., pp. 167–201.

22 Marriott, Oliver, *The Property Boom*, Pan, 1969, p. 306.

23 Quoted in Berry, Brian (ed.), *City Classification Handbook*, Wiley, 1972, p. 225.

24 See Briggs, Asa, *Victorian Cities*, Penguin, 1968, p. 31.

25 See Green, L. P., *Provincial Metropolis*, Allen & Unwin, 1959.

26 Coppock, J. T., 'Dormitory Settlements around London', in Coppock, J. T. and Prince, H. C., op. cit., p. 275.

27 Thomas, D., 'The Green Belt', in Coppock, J. T. and Prince, H. C., op. cit., p. 311.

28 Hall, Peter, *et al.*, *The Containment of Urban England*, 2 vols., Allen & Unwin/Sage, 1973.

29 Quoted in Best, Robin H., 'New Towns in the London Region', in Coppock, J. T. and Prince, H. C., op. cit., p. 316.

30 See Craven, E., 'Private Residential Expansion in Kent 1956–64', *Urban Studies*, vol. 6, 1969.

31 Pahl, R. E., *Readings in Urban Sociology*, Pergamon, 1968, p. 263.

32 Ash, Maurice, *A Guide to the Structure of London*, Adams & Dart, 1972.

33 Pahl, R. E., op. cit., p. 273.

34 Quoted in Hillman, Judy, 'The Deep End of the Pool', *Guardian*, 15 September 1972.

35 *Royal Commission on Local Government in England* (Cmnd 4040), 1969, vol. II, p. 165.

36 James, Henry, *English Hours*, Heinemann, 1962, p. 124.

Chapter Two

1 Dyos, H. J. and Wolff, M., op. cit.

2 Quoted by Glass, Ruth in Pahl, R. E., op. cit., p. 65.

References

3 Williams-Ellis, Clough (ed.), *Britain and the Beast*, Dent, 1938.

4 Boulding, Kenneth E., in Handlin, O. and Burchard, J. (ed.), *The Historian and the City*, Cambridge, Mass., 1963.

5 A fascinating exploration of this theme is provided by Raymond Williams in his *The Country and the City*, Chatto & Windus, 1973.

6 Pahl, R. E., op. cit., p. 136.

7 Doxiadis, C. A., *Between Dystopia and Utopia*, Faber, 1968.

8 Handlin, O. and Burchard, J., op. cit., p. 7.

9 Geddes, Patrick, op. cit., p. 27.

10 ibid., p. 49.

11 See Mumford, Lewis, *The Urban Prospect*, Secker & Warburg, 1968.

12 Rodwin, Lloyd, op. cit., pp. 153–5.

13 Hall, Peter, *et al.*, op. cit.

14 Jacobs, Jane, *The Economy of Cities*, Cape, 1970.

15 Elkins, T. H., *The Urban Explosion*, Macmillan, 1973, p. 39.

16 Cullingworth, J. B., *Problems of an Urban Society*, vol. I *The Social Framework of Planning*, Allen & Unwin, 1972, pp. 86–92.

17 Patmore, Allan, *Land and Leisure*, Penguin, 1972, pp. 115–16.

18 Best, R. H. and Coppock, J. T., *The Changing Use of Land in Britain*, Faber, 1962, p. 229 and Best, R. H., 'Land Conversions to Urban Use', *Social Science Research Council Newsletter*, 19 June 1973.

19 Patmore, Allan, op. cit., p. 133.

20 Cullingworth, J. B., op. cit. Chs. 2 and 3 bring together much of the evidence on recent population trends and urban growth policies.

21 Mumford, op. cit.

22 Doxiadis, op. cit., p. 59.

23 ibid.

24 ibid., p. 74.

Chapter Three

1 *Royal Commission on Local Government in England* (Cmnd 4040), vol. II, 1969.

2 Foster, John, 'Nineteenth Century Towns, a Class Dimension', in Dyos, H. J. (ed.), op. cit., 1968, pp. 281–300.

3 Hennock, E. P., *Fit and Proper Persons*, Edward Arnold, 1973, p. 312–13.

4 Jones, G. W., *Borough Politics*, Macmillan, 1969, p. 150.

5 ibid., p. 348.

6 ibid., p. 348.
7 Hennock, E. P., op. cit., p. 333.
8 Briggs, Asa, op. cit., p. 254.
9 Jones, G. W., op. cit., p. 33.
10 Clarke, P. F., *Lancashire and the New Liberalism*, Cambridge University Press, 1971.
11 Lee, J. M., *Social Leaders and Public Persons*, Oxford University Press, 1963.
12 Hennock, E. P. in Dyos, H. J. (ed.), op. cit., 1968, p. 317.
13 Jones, G. W., op. cit., pp. 351–89.
14 ibid., p. 186.
15 ibid., p. 229.
16 Eversley, David, in Dyos, H. J. (ed.), op. cit., 1968.
17 Jones, G. W., op. cit., p. 230.
18 Berry, Brian, *The Human Consequences of Urbanisation*, Macmillan, 1973, p. 165.
19 Dahl, Robert A., *After the Revolution?*, Yale, 1970, p. 154.

Part Two

Chapter One

1 Williams, Oliver P., *Metropolitan Political Analysis*, Free Press, 1971, p. 110.
2 Donnison, D. V., quoted in Spencer, K., 'Housing and Socially Deprived Families', Holman, Robert (ed.), *Socially Deprived Families in Britain*, Bedford Square Press, 1970, p. 65.
3 See, e.g. Parker, R. A., *The Housing Finance Bill and Council Tenants*, Child Poverty Action Group, Poverty Pamphlet 9; Goudie, J., *Councils and the Housing Finance Act*, Young Fabian Pamphlet no. 31.
4 Wendt, P., *Housing Policy, the Search for Solutions*, University of California Press, 1962, p. 269.
5 ibid., p. 26.
6 Cullingworth, J. B., *Housing in Transition: a Case Study in the City of Lancaster*, Heinemann, 1963.
7 *Report of the Committee on Housing in Greater London*, Milner-Holland Report, HMSO, 1965.
8 *Scotland's Older Houses*, Scottish Housing Advisory Committee, HMSO, 1967.

References

9 Parker, R. A., *The Rents of Council Houses*, Bell, 1967.
10 'Mr Crosland Joins the Retreat', *Guardian*, 7 June 1974.
11 *Council Housing: Purposes, Procedures and Priorities*, Central Housing Advisory Committee, HMSO, 1969. See discussion in Cullingworth, J. B., *Problems of an Urban Society*, vol. II, Allen & Unwin, 1972, pp. 38–68.
12 Cullingworth, J. B., op. cit., 1972, p. 52.
13 Parker, R. A., op. cit., p. 72.
14 Cullingworth, J. B., op. cit., 1972, p. 54.
15 Donnison, D. V., quoted in Spencer, K., op. cit., p. 65.
16 Spencer, K., op. cit., p. 99.
17 Stone, P. A., *Urban Development in Britain: Standards, Costs and Resources*, Cambridge University Press, 1970.
18 Such as, e.g. Carey, Lynnette and Mapes, Roy, *The Sociology of Planning*, Batsford, 1972.
19 Cullingworth, J. B., op. cit., 1972, p. 82.
20 *The Deeplish Study*, Ministry of Housing and Local Government, HMSO, 1966.
21 *London's Housing Needs*, London Council of Social Science, 1973.
22 Stone, P. A., op. cit., p. 273.
23 *Guardian*, 19 November, 1974.

Chapter Two

1 Cullingworth, J. B., op. cit., 1972, p. 21.
2 Spencer, K., op. cit., p. 108.
3 Taken from Holman, R., op. cit., p. 218–19.
4 Hatch, S. and Sherrott, R., 'Positive Discrimination and the Distribution of Deprivation', *Policy and Politics*, vol. 1, 1973. See also Lomas, Graham, in Donnison, D. V. and Eversley, D. (eds.), *London: Urban Problems, Patterns and Policies*, Heinemann, 1973, pp. 51–85.
5 Barnes, J. H., 'A Solution to Whose Problem?', Glennester, H. and Hatch, S., *Positive Discrimination and Inequality*, Fabian Research Series, 314, 1974.
6 Holman, R., op. cit., pp. 175–84.
7 *Guardian*, 9 September 1974.
8 *A New Approach to the Problems of Cities*, Shelter, March 1972.
9 Dearlove, John, *The Politics of Policy in Local Government*, Cambridge University Press, 1973.
10 *The New Granby Centre and S.N.A.P. Liverpool*, Shelter, 1972, p. 12.
11 'No Party for the Poor', *Guardian*, 2 April 1974.

12 In Donnison, D. V. and Eversley, D., op. cit., pp. 44–50.
13 See Part Three, Chapter 1.
14 Sennett, Richard, *The Uses of Disorder*, Allen Lane, 1971.
15 Medhurst, F. and Lewis, J. Parry, *Urban Decay*, Macmillan, 1969, p. 20.

Part Three

Chapter One

1 Quoted in Hennock, E. P., *Fit and Proper Persons*, Edward Arnold, 1973, p. 172.
2 *The New Local Authorities: Management and Structure*, Bains Report, HMSO, 1972, para. 4.33.
3 Robson, W. A., 'Local and Regional Government', B. Crick (ed.), *Essays on Reform: a Centenary Tribute*, Oxford University Press, 1967, p. 162.
4 Stanyer, J., 'The Royal Commission on Local Government', in Chapman, Richard A., *The Role of Royal Commissions in Policy-Making*, Allen & Unwin, 1973, pp. 105–42.
5 Much of it is drawn together in Hill, Dilys, *Democratic Theory and Local Government* (Allen & Unwin, 1974), which unfortunately appeared too late to be taken account of in this volume.
6 Quoted in Sharpe, L. J., 'Theories and Values of Local Government', *Political Studies*, 18, 1970, p. 153.
7 Boaden, N. T., 'Innovation and Change in English Local Government', *Political Studies*, 1971, pp. 416–29.
8 Money, W. J., 'The Need to Sustain a Viable System of Local Democracy', *Urban Studies*, vol. 10, 1973.
9 Sharpe, L. J., op. cit., pp. 153–74.
10 ibid., p. 168.
11 Quoted in Clements, Roger V., *Local Notables and the City Council*, Macmillan, 1969, p. 17.
12 *Report of the Committee on the Management of Local Government*, Maud Report, HMSO, 1967, vol. I, p. 84.
13 *Royal Commission on Local Government* (Short Version), (Cmnd 4040), HMSO, 1969, p. 16.
14 Hennock, E. P., op. cit.
15 ibid.
16 See Part One, Chapter 3.

References

17 Heclo, H., 'The Councillor's Job', *Public Administration*, 47, 1969, pp. 185–202.
18 ibid., p. 193.
19 ibid., p. 189.
20 ibid., p. 189.
21 Walsh, A. H., *The Urban Challenge to Government*, Praeger, 1969, p. 29.
22 See e.g. Blondel, J. and Hall, R., 'Conflict, Decision-Making and the Perceptions of Local Councillors', *Political Studies*, vol. 15, 1967, pp. 322–30.
23 See Rees, A., and Smith, T., *Town Councillors*, Action Society Trust, 1964.
24 Hampton, William, *Democracy and Community*, Oxford University Press, 1970, p. 284.
25 Boaden, N. T., *Urban Policy-Making*, Cambridge University Press, 1971, pp. 112–15.
26 Hampton, op. cit., p. 242.
27 See Heclo, op. cit.
28 Maud Report, op. cit., vol. II, pp. 89–164.
29 Clements, op. cit., p. 53.
30 ibid., p. 58.
31 Self, P., 'Elected Representatives and Management in Local Government; an Alternative Analysis', *Public Administration*, 49, 1971, pp. 269–78.
32 Stanyer, J., 'Elected Representatives and Management in Local Government', *Public Administration*, 49, 1971, pp. 73–87.
33 Self, op. cit., p. 273.
34 Bains Report, op. cit. See also Jones, G. W., 'The Function and Organisation of Councillors', *Public Administration*, 51, 1973.
35 Woodham, J. B., 'Management and Local Democracy', *Local Government Studies*, vol. 2, 1972, pp. 13–21.
36 *New Society*, 27 December, 1973, p. 762.
37 Stewart, J. D., 'Corporate Planning: the Councillor Must Take Control', *Municipal Review*, 531, 1974, p. 446.
38 Jones, G. W., *Borough Politics*, Macmillan, 1969, p. 226.
39 Bains Report, op. cit., Ch. 4.
40 Greenwood, R., Norton, A. C. and Stewart, J. D., 'Recent Reforms in the Internal Organisation of County Boroughs', *Inlogov Occasional Paper*, Series A, no. 1.
41 Stewart, J. D., *Management in Local Government*, Charles Knight, 1971, p. 167.

42 See Elliott, J., 'The Harris Experiment at Newcastle upon Tyne', *Public Administration*, 49, 1971, pp. 149–62; and Wright, D. S., 'The City Manager as a Development Administrator', in Daland, Robert A., *Comparative Urban Research*, Sage, 1969, pp. 203–48.

43 Quoted by Elliott, ibid., p. 153.

44 Bains Report, op. cit., Ch. 5.

45 Greenwood *et al.*, op. cit., p. 49.

46 See Stewart, J. D., op. cit., 1971, *passim*; Friend, J. K., and Jessop, W. N., *Local Government and Strategic Choice*, Tavistock, 1969.

47 Stewart, J. D., op. cit., 1971, p. 124.

48 Stewart, J. D., op. cit., 1974, p. 446.

49 Mill, J. S., *On Representative Government*, Everyman, 1960, p. 356.

50 Self, P., op. cit.

Chapter Two

1 Walsh, A. H., op. cit., p. 123.

2 Marshall, A. H., *New Revenues for Local Government*, Fabian Research Series, 295, 1971, p. 25.

3 ibid., p. 27.

4 Boaden, N. T., op. cit., 1971, *passim*.

5 Davey, K. J., 'Local Autonomy and Independent Revenues', *Public Administration*, 49, 1971, pp. 45–50.

6 Marshall, A. H., *Financial Management in Local Government*, Allen & Unwin, 1974, p. 20.

7 'Rates Grant a Boon to Others', *Guardian*, 30 May 1974.

8 Marshall, A. H., op. cit., 1971.

9 Royal Institute of Public Administration. *Sources of Local Revenue* (Allen & Unwin, 1956), and *New Sources of Local Revenue* (1968).

10 Kirwan, R., 'The Contribution of Public Expenditure and Finance to the Problems of Inner London', in Donnison, D. V. and Eversley, D., *London: Problems, Patterns and Policies*, Heinemann, 1973, pp. 119–55.

11 *Local Income Tax as a Source of Local Government Finance*, Institute of Municipal Treasurers and Accountants, 1968.

12 Kirwan, R., op. cit.

13 Marshall, A. H., op. cit., 1971, p. 5.

14 Maynard, Alan K., and King, David N., *Rates or Prices*, Institute of Economic Affairs, *Hobart Paper*, 54.

References

15 *The Future Shape of Local Government Finance* (Cmnd 4741), HMSO, 1971.
16 The Layfield Committee was still receiving evidence at the time of going to press. In its evidence, the Labour party endorsed the removal of teachers' salaries to the Exchequer, and proposed that water and sewerage should cease to be a local charge; but it recommended the retention of the rates, unless there were to be a further reform of local government.
17 Kirwan, R., op. cit., p. 129.

Part Four

Chapter One

1 Mill, J. S., op. cit., p. 247.
2 Crossman, R. H. S., 'Towards a Philosophy of Socialism', Crossman, R. H. S. (ed.), *New Fabian Essays*, Fabian Society, 1952.
3 Thoenies, Piet, *The Élite in the Welfare State*, Faber, 1966, pp. 190–91.
4 Altschuler, Alan A., *The Urban Planning Process*, Cornell University Press, 1965, p. 375.
5 Walsh, A. H., *The Urban Challenge to Government*, Praeger, 1969, p. 29.
6 Altschuler, op. cit., p. 405.
7 See e.g. Levin, Peter, 'Opening up the Planning Process', in Hatch, Stephen, *Towards Participation in Local Services*, Fabian Tract, 419, 1973, pp. 16–28.
8 Downs, Anthony, *Inside Bureaucracy*, Rand, 1964, pp. 175–90.
9 Much of this may be illuminated by the diaries of R. H. S. Crossman.
10 Nisbet, Robert A., *Tradition and Revolt*, Vintage Books, 1970, p. 198.

Chapter Two

1 Nisbet, Robert A., *Community and Power*, Oxford University Press, 1962, p. 274.
2 Quoted in Dennis, N., *People and Planning*, Faber, 1970, p. 303.
3 See especially Dennis, N., op. cit. and *Public Participation and Planning Blight*, Faber, 1972. See also 'Planned Redevelopment

and Public Participation in Sunderland', *Southwestern Review of Public Administration*, no. 10, 1971.

4 Dennis, N., op. cit., 1970, p. 173.
5 ibid., p. 182.
6 ibid., p. 251.
7 ibid., p. 231.
8 ibid., p. 267.
9 ibid., p. 271.
10 ibid., p. 322.
11 Dennis, N., 'The Duke Street Story', *New Society*, 4 October 1973, pp. 6–10.
12 Davies, Jon Gower, *The Evangelistic Bureaucrat*, Tavistock, 1972.
13 By Dennis.
14 Banfield, Edward C., *Urban Renewal and the Planners, Policy and Politics*, vol. 1, 1972, pp. 163–9.
15 Dennis, N., op. cit., 1972, p. 238.

Chapter Three

1 Eversley, David, paper at British Association. August 1971.
2 Altschuler, op. cit., p. 351.
3 ibid., p. 409.
4 Reade, Eric, 'Some Notes Towards a Sociology of Planning', *Journal of the Town Planning Institute*, 54, 1968, pp. 214–18.
5 Dennis, N., op. cit., 1970, p. 329.
6 Toffler, Alvin, *Future Shock*, Pan, pp. 11–12.
7 Quoted in Davies, Jon G., op. cit., p. 110.
8 ibid., p. 222.
9 Cherry, G. E., *Town Planning in its Social Context*, L. Hill, 1970, p. 177.
10 Eversley, David, in Donnison, D. V. and Eversley, D. (eds.), op. cit., p. 5.
11 Cullingworth, J. B., op. cit., p. 184.
12 Gans, Herbert J., *People and Plans*, Basic Books, 1968.
13 Senior, Derek, in Cowan, Peter (ed.), *The Future of Planning*, Heinemann, 1973, p. 127.
14 Gans, Herbert J., op. cit., p. 80.
15 Eversley, David, *The Planner in Society*, Faber, 1973.
16 Eversley, David, op. cit., 1971.
17 Dennis, N., op. cit., 1972, p. 278.
18 Eversley, David, in Donnison, D. V. and Eversley, D., op. cit., p. 3.

References

19 Rawls, John, *A Theory of Justice*, Oxford University Press, 1972, p. 230.
20 Dahl, Robert A., *After the Revolution?*, Yale, 1970.

Part Five

Chapter One

1 Grimond, Jo, 'Community Politics', *Government and Opposition*, 7, 1972, p. 135.
2 Moore, Barrington, *Reflections on the Causes of Human Misery*, Allen Lane, 1972, p. 67.
3 See contributions by Grimond, J., Barker, A., and Parry, G. in *Government and Opposition*, 7, 1972; and Parry, G. (ed.), *Participation*, Manchester University Press, 1972.
4 Thompson, Dennis F., *The Democratic Citizen*, Cambridge University Press, 1970.
5 Pateman, Carole, *Participation and Democratic Theory*, Cambridge University Press, 1970.
6 Almond, G. and Verba, S., *The Civic Culture*, Princeton University Press, 1963.
7 Dahl, Robert A., *After the Revolution?*, Yale University Press, 1970, p. 162.
8 Rowland, Jon, *Community Decay*, Penguin, 1973.
9 ibid., p. 137.
10 ibid., p. 146.
11 See Parry, G., 'All Power to the Community', *European Journal of Sociology*, vol. XIII, 1972, pp. 126–38.
12 Barker, A., 'Communities and "Normal Politics"', *Government and Opposition*, 7, 1972, p. 159.
13 Goldthorpe, J. H. *et al.*, *The Affluent Worker: Political Attitudes & Behaviour*, Cambridge University Press, 1968.
14 Pahl, R. E., *Patterns of Urban Life*, Longman, 1970, pp. 88–9.
15 Walsh, A. H., *The Urban Challenge to Government*, Praeger, 1969, p. 21.
16 Bachrach, P., and Baratz, M., *Power and Poverty*, Oxford University Press, 1970, p. 201ff.
17 Dearlove, John, *The Politics of Policy in Local Government*, Cambridge University Press, 1972.
18 Bachrach, P., and Baratz, M., op. cit., p. 44.

19 Parry, G. in Parry, G. (ed.), op. cit., 1972, p. 35.
20 Thompson, D., op. cit., p. 57.

Chapter Two

1 Gans, Herbert J., op. cit., p. ix.
2 Cullingworth, J. B., op. cit., 1972, p. 169.
3 Walsh, A. H., op. cit., p. 21.
4 *People and Planning in Manchester*, Department of Adult Education, Manchester University, 1970.
5 'The Public Case Heard but not Seen', *Guardian*, July 1974.
6 Elkin, Stephen L., *Politics and Land-Use Planning*, Cambridge
   University Press, 1974.
7 Jay, A., *The Householder's Guide to Community Defence against
   Bureaucratic Aggression*, Cape, 1972.
8 Levin, Peter, 'Opening up the Planning Process', in Hatch,
   Stephen, *Towards Participation in Local Services*, Fabian Tract
   419, 1973, p. 27.
9 Jay, A., op. cit., p. 7.
10 Report of the Committee on Public Participation in Planning,
   People and Planning, Skeffington Report, HMSO, 1969.
11 *Guardian*, 31 December 1969.
12 *Architect's Journal*, 6 August 1969.
13 Senior, Derek, 'Planning and the Public', Cowan, T. (ed.), op. cit.,
   p. 123.
14 *Structure Plans: the Examination in Public*, HMSO, 1973, p. 7.
15 Zetter, R., 'Towards Less Participation in Planning', *New Society*,
   9 August 1973, pp. 331–4.
16 ibid., p. 334.
17 Crick, Bernard, and Green, G., 'People and Planning', *New
   Society*, 5 September 1968.
18 Gans, H. J., 'The Levittowners', Allen Lane, 1967, p. xl.
19 Eversley, David, *The Planner in Society*, Faber, 1973.
20 Town & Country Planning Association, *Planning Aid Service:
   Report of the First Year*, 1973–4, p. 3.
21 Sponsored by Mr William Mulloy, MP. The bill was of course lost
   with the dissolution in September 1974.
22 Cullingworth, J. B., op. cit., p. 168.

Chapter Three

1 See Cox, Harvey and Morgan, David, *City Politics and the Press*,
   Cambridge University Press, 1974.

References

2 Seymour-Ure, Colin, *The Political Impact of Mass Media*, Constable, 1974.
3 *Guardian*, 3 May 1974.
4 See Burke, Roger, *The Murky Cloak: Local Authority Press Relations*, Charles Knight, 1970.
5 See Hill, Dilys, *Democratic Theory and Local Government*, Allen & Unwin, 1974, pp. 179–84.

Chapter Four

1 Donnison, David, Donnison, D. V. and Eversley, D., op. cit., 1973, p. 384.
2 Dahl, Robert A., 'The City in the Future of Democracy', *American Political Science Review*, vol. LXI, 1967, p. 959.
3 Nisbet, Robert, op. cit., 1962, p. xi.
4 Dennis, Norman, 'The Popularity of the Neighbourhood Community Idea', Pahl, R. E. (ed.), *Readings in Urban Sociology*, Pergamon, 1968, p. 75.
5 *Royal Commission on Local Government in England* (Cmnd 4040), HMSO, 1969 (Redcliffe-Maud Report), vol. II, 'Memorandum of Dissent by Mr D. Senior', para. 449.
6 Morton, Jane, 'Parish Pumps Revived', *New Society*, 29 January 1970, pp. 173–4.
7 *Royal Commission on Local Government in England* (Cmnd 4040), HMSO, 1969, vol. III, *Research Appendix*, 8, 'Parish Councils', pp. 165–96.
8 Morton, Jane, op. cit.
9 *Royal Commission on Local Government in England* (Cmnd 4040), HMSO, 1969, vol. III, *Research Appendix*, 8, para. 84, p. 193.
10 See Wood, Robert C., *Suburbia*, Houghton Mifflin, 1958; and Wood, Robert C., *1400 Governments*, Harvard University Press, 1961.
11 Information kindly supplied through the office of the mayor of Indianapolis.
12 Redcliffe-Maud Report, vol. II, para. 430, p. 127.
13 ibid., para. 444, p. 131.
14 *Royal Commission on Local Government in England* (Cmnd 4040), HMSO, 1969, vol. III, *Research Appendix*, 7, pp. 129–65.
15 Hampton, William, *Democracy and Community*, Oxford University Press, pp. 98–121.
16 *The Housing Plan: a Case for Neighbourhood Councils*, National Suggestions Centre, 1970.

17 Hampton, William and Chapman, J. J., 'Towards Neighbourhood Councils', *Political Quarterly*, vol. 42, 1971, pp. 247–54, 414–22.

18 The Hornsey Plan, op. cit.

19 See for example, Drake, Charles D., 'Ombudsmen for Local Government', *Public Administration*, 48, 1970, pp. 179–89.

20 Stacey, Frank, *The British Ombudsman*, Oxford University Press, 1971.

21 Quoted in ibid., p. 315.

Index

More about Penguins and Pelicans

Penguinews, which appears every month, contains details of all the new books issued by Penguins as they are published. From time to time it is supplemented by *Penguins in Print*, which is our complete list of almost 5,000 titles.

A specimen copy of *Penguinews* will be sent to you free on request. Please write to Dept EP, Penguin Books Ltd, Harmondsworth, Middlesex, for your copy.

In the U.S.A.: For a complete list of books available from Penguins in the United States write to Dept CS, Penguin Books, 625 Madison Avenue, New York, New York 10022.

In Canada: For a complete list of books available from Penguins in Canada write to Penguin Books Canada Ltd, 2801 John Street, Markham, Ontario L3R 1B4.

Changing Britain: Two classics of sociology

Michael Young and Peter Willmott

FAMILY AND KINSHIP IN EAST LONDON

The two authors of this most human of surveys are sociologists.

They spent three years on 'field work' in Bethnal Green, London, and on a new housing estate in Essex. The result is a fascinating study, made during a period of extensive rehousing, of family and community ties and the pull of the 'wider family' on working-class people. Since its first publication their report has come to be recognized as a classic of modern sociology.

THE SYMMETRICAL FAMILY

'In their most ambitious book to date the directors of the Institute of Community Studies have analysed 2,644 interviews with inhabitants of twenty-four local authority areas in the London Metropolitan Region to discover how we spend our lives, what hours we give to work and leisure, and the effects that the changing patterns of work, leisure, technology and social class are having on the form of the contemporary family, how this differs from what we can discern of the past and what we may expect future trends to be. Like all the work of this institute the sample is statistically satisfactory and is handled with sophistication . . . a major addition to our knowledge of English life today' – *Observer*

Charles Mercer

LIVING IN CITIES

Psychology and the Urban Environment

The evolution of the city – from the Greek *polis* to the modern conurbation – has provided man with both a source of beauty and inspiration, and a set of social, economic and organizational problems that increase as the population swells.

Charles Mercer attempts to clarify the effect that environment has on man and the ways in which man, in turn, influences the environment. As an environmental psychologist, he adopts a different approach from the geographer, architect or sociologist and asks such questions as 'to what extent are people shaped by buildings and towns?', 'is overcrowding damaging?' and 'how do different environments foster or hinder community?'. These he relates to the conclusions drawn from studies carried out in laboratories and cities and builds up a composite picture of how men and women react to the pressures of living in cities.

K. H. Schaeffer and Elliot Sclar

ACCESS FOR ALL

Transportation and Urban Growth

Our cities are being strangled by the technology that made them possible. In *Access for All* two American experts examine the problem through historical analysis and specific case history. They argue that while improved transport enabled the horrifically overcrowded cities of the last century to expand and attain a balance between individual privacy and the economies of scale, the same process resulted in a growth and dispersion of the urban areas which led individuals, in their search for privacy, to lose the concept of community.